TOTAL MARKETING

CAPTURING CUSTOMERS WITH MARKETING PLANS THAT WORK

TOTAL MARKETING
CAPTURING CUSTOMERS WITH MARKETING PLANS THAT WORK

Don Debelak

Dow Jones-Irwin
Homewood, Illinois 60430

Sponsoring editor: *Susan Glinert Stevens, Ph.D.*
Project editor: *Rita McMullen*
Production manager: *Ann Cassady*
Jacket Designer: *Ray Machura*
Compositor: *Publication Services*
Typeface: *11/ 13 Times Roman*
Printer: *R. R. Donnelley & Sons Company*

Library of Congress Cataloging-in-Publication Data

Debelak, Don.
   Total marketing : capturing customers with marketing plans that
work / Don Debelak.
     p.   cm.
   Includes Index.
   ISBN 1-55623-192-X
   1. Marketing—Management. I. Title.
HF5415.13.D377 1989
658.8—dc19

                                            89–30049
                                            CIP

Printed in the United States of America
1 2 3 4 5 6 7 8 9 0 DO 6 5 4 3 2 1 0 9

CONTENTS

CHAPTER 1

MARKETING—HOW TO GET STARTED

People have always been fascinated with marketing success stories, and many of these stories have become modern legends. Some examples are: Apple's success in personal computers, McDonald's growth in the fast-food industry, Ford's introduction of the Mustang, Miller Brewing's market inroads with Miller Lite, IBM's dominance in mainframe computers, and Budweiser's control of the beer market.

People are equally delighted by marketing failures: the introduction of the Edsel, IBM PC Jr. computers, and new Coke—all examples of resounding marketing disasters.

The results of marketing moves can be astounding. Companies' fortunes can be made or lost. A telling example is General Motors, the grandfather of modern marketing strategy. In the early 1920s, Ford mass-produced Model Ts and dominated the car market. General Motors determined that customers would like cars that reflected their owners' economic statuses: Chevrolets for the average buyer, Buicks for the more upscale buyer, and Cadillacs for the rich buyer. This strategic marketing move paved the way for General Motors' rise to an industrial giant.

General Motors' marketing strategy created a demand for its cars by finding a marketing tactic that differentiated its cars from the competition in a way that was important to the customer.

Notice that I did not use the traditional statement that a marketer creates demand by satisfying customer needs. Satisfying customer needs is important, but that alone is not going to help a marketer if 10 other companies are satisfying customers' needs in the same way. A marketer not only must satisfy a need, but satisfy it in a way that is unique. In the General Motors example, both General Motors and Ford met the customer's need for transportation. General Motors' strategy was unique because its cars also reflected the customer's economic status.

1

Finding a unique way to meet customer needs is not easy. That is why a marketing plan is important. A marketer can find a unique marketing strategy while analyzing a business in the marketing plan process.

Is the General Motors example missing something? Does the example talk about an advertising campaign, a public relations campaign, or a promotion campaign? No. Nor does the example include any implementation tactics. An effective marketing plan first develops a meaningful strategy and then develops effective implementation tactics.

WHEN DO MARKETING PLANS WORK?

Marketing plans work when they are based on unique, meaningful marketing strategies—strategies based on key marketing elements that are important to customers.

To be a successful marketer you need to be able to determine the key marketing elements for your business; however, I can't give you a rigid formula for doing this. Every business has different problems, opportunities, customers, and objectives. Dozens of factors could be key marketing elements for a business.

To help you find the key marketing element of your business, I can show you how to analyze your business from a marketing perspective. I can walk you through all the aspects of a business that should be analyzed from a marketing perspective. And I can use a steady stream of examples to help you discover the marketing aspects that apply to your business.

The goal of this book is to give you a framework for writing an effective marketing plan. I hope to get you to think about your business, evaluate what your customers really want, and determine what your product really has to offer. I want to help you find ways to improve your marketing methods. Most people have a good, intuitive knowledge of their business and customers. I hope to help you use this knowledge along with marketing principles to develop successful marketing strategies and plans.

KEY MARKETING ELEMENTS

You must know what the key marketing elements are in your business in order to develop an effective marketing plan. What is a key marketing element? The answer lies in the definition of marketing.

Marketing is the process of creating a link between customers and products. The link is created by generating customer demand for a product and by placing the product into the market so the customer can buy it.

A key marketing element is any aspect of a business that is capable of strengthening the link between a product and its customers. In the General Motors example, the key marketing element was customers' desires to have their cars reflect their economic status.

WHO IS THE BOOK FOR?

This book is written for (1) the businessperson who wants to improve his or her company's marketing but doesn't know how to do it; (2) the person who has just transferred into a marketing position but isn't sure how to create a marketing program; (3) the entrepreneur who has been told by venture capitalists that he or she needs a marketing plan in order to obtain financing; (4) the professional who wants to learn how to incorporate marketing techniques into his or her practice; and (5) the person who works for a big company and wants to know just what the company president meant when she said the company was going to become marketing oriented.

This book is designed so a person can start reading it on Monday and finish a marketing plan by Friday. The book is full of practical advice that is straightforward and easy to understand. I've tried to translate complex marketing phrases, such as psychographic market segmentation, into simpler concepts, such as understanding your customer's personality.

This book shows you how to write a marketing plan, but the book offers more than just a marketing plan format. It discusses how the aspects of marketing can relate to a business. While discussing the aspects of marketing, I explain what marketing is, what key marketing elements are, and in what situations certain marketing strategies and tactics will work. After you finish the book, you should have an understanding of what marketing is all about.

WHY A BOOK ON PLANNING?

At my first marketing job, a manager came back from a seminar on positioning and declared, "We have to position our chemical line. George, our top salesperson, told me he never loses a sale when he convinces customers that we have better technical backup than our competitors. That should be our campaign next year." After that program failed, the sales department insisted on a price discount program. Sales rose 15 percent but profits fell 5 percent.

Most marketing plans are developed by this kind of trial and error process. Consider Burger King. I can picture the marketing "war room." "Wendy's is killing us with the old lady. We need to get a goofy guy." The result was the quickly dropped "Herb" program, where Burger King looked for the one person—Herb—who had never visited a Burger King.

Advertising, public relations, positioning, promotion, and telemarketing are all topics covered extensively in books and magazines. But implementing a program is only half the marketing challenge; analyzing the market to develop a profitable marketing strategy is the other half. Without doing both, a businessperson is not going to hit his or her profit targets.

Mitsubishi ran a TV ad campaign on its Mirage cars. In the ad, a family drives around in a Mirage. A series of people pull up next to the car at stop signs, look at the Mirage, and say, "Nice car." At the end of the ad, the slogan "Suddenly the obvious choice" is used. Mitsubishi's implementation tactics were adequate, but Mitsubishi did a terrible job analyzing potential customers. Mitsubishi's problem is that most people don't know about Mitsubishi cars. The questions that most need to be answered are: What is a Mitsubishi, and why should I buy one? Implementation that's not based on a meaningful plan won't produce positive results.

Marketing is an activity with many diverse tasks. It is difficult to analyze a business's marketing efforts without a structure that covers every aspect of marketing. At the same time, every consumer is exposed to marketing every day. Most people have a reaction to marketing campaigns. Many people mistakenly believe this exposure alone can teach them about marketing. But a little knowledge can be dangerous. Too often marketers develop a plan by considering only 25 to 50 percent of the marketing picture. That's the purpose of this book—to help a businessperson understand the total marketing perspective.

THE BOOK'S FORMAT

The book's format follows the four key steps in developing a marketing plan:

1. Analyzing a business from a marketing perspective to find key marketing elements that are important to the company's customers.
2. Creating a meaningful marketing strategy that focuses on important key marketing elements.
3. Developing implementation tactics that both enhance the strategy and communicate the strategy effectively to the customer.
4. Writing the marketing plan that includes a timetable for a business to follow throughout the year.

The following quick look at each chapter shows how the book builds from the definition "marketing is creating a link between customers and products" to the final completion of an effective marketing plan.

Analyzing Your Business from a Marketing Perspective (Chapters 2–6)

Chapter 2: Customers: Who are they? What are they like? Why do they buy, and why don't they buy? What is important to them, and what do they think of your product?

Chapter 3: The product: How to understand it. How to position it. How to price it. How to turn it into a customer solution. How to improve its perceived value.

Chapter 4: Placement: Getting your product to the customer. Why it's the most overlooked aspect of marketing. How to determine if you have the right placement strategy. How to make your placement strategies more effective.

Chapter 5: Survival issues: Profitable pricing, defensibility, and momentum are the key marketing elements that determine if you will stay in business.

Chapter 6: What's happening today? What is your current market situation? What will your competitors do next? How to use long-term strategies to solve short-term problems.

Creating and Implementing Your Marketing Strategy (Chapters 7–9)

Chapter 7: Choosing your marketing strategy: The right and wrong way to choose a strategy. Examples of companies that chose effective strategies and examples of companies that chose ineffective strategies. Possible strategies for tough marketing problems.

Chapter 8:   Communicating your strategy: How to enhance and effectively communicate your strategy. When to use various implementation tactics and how to make them work effectively.

Chapter 9:   Inside-out marketing: How to build your program from the ground up. How to have every aspect of your business reflect your strategy. How to focus on the customer. How professional practices can use inside-out marketing tactics.

Writing the Plan (Chapters 10–13)

Chapter 10:   The marketing plan format: What it is and why it's that way. How to make the plan work for you.

Chapter 11:   Plans of successful companies: McDonald's—strategies that McDonald's uses to stay on top in the fast-food industry. Hitachi VCRs—strategies to keep a VCR manufacturer profitable as a market matures.

Chapter 12:   Plans of struggling companies: Technical Test Products—a small test equipment company struggles to survive in a market where technology is changing. Party goods paper outlet—a store needs to reposition itself to survive against a larger competitor. Dental practice—a young dentist tries to rejuvenate a retiring dentist's practice.

Chapter 13:   Plans of new companies: Physical therapy equipment—two engineers introduce a new product in a market with five established competitors. Specialized consulting service—two entrepreneurs plan to establish credibility in order to create a customer base. Plumbing service—an out-of-work plumber starts his own business with $2,000.

HOW TO BEST USE THE BOOK

The best way to do a marketing plan is to step away from your normal business activities for a day or two, forget all your immediate problems, and try to analyze your business objectively. The best way to use this book is to set aside a block of time and use this book as a checklist in your planning process.

Chapters 2–6 cover analyzing your business from a marketing perspective. As you read the sections, ask yourself: Does this apply to my business? Are my current marketing programs dealing with this topic effectively? Are my competitors doing a better job of addressing this issue? Is this an area that could be the basis for my marketing strategy?

Chapter 7 covers methods that can be used for creating a marketing strategy. As you read the strategy examples, check off the ones that look like they will apply to your business. Write down any strategies that you might want to use in your own marketing plan.

After you finish reading the examples, you will need to choose potential marketing strategies. After you have selected a few strategies based upon your business's key marketing elements, evaluate them with the marketing strategy checklist to determine how effective your strategies will be.

Chapters 8 and 9 cover implementation tactics. Again, the topics covered can serve as a checklist. Decide which tactics will work best for your business, and read how to implement those tactics effectively.

Finally, Chapters 10–13 contain the marketing plan format and eight sample marketing plans. When reading these plans, look for ideas or tactics that might fit your business. Once you have finished the book, you will be ready to go back to Chapter 10 and follow the marketing plan format while writing your own plan.

MARKETING INTUITION

Up to now I may have given the impression that marketing can be a predictable activity, which is not the case. In fact, what makes marketing so exciting is its inexactness. You can't just enter a market, pull out marketing theories, and expect to be successful. Marketing calls for an intuitive understanding of your product, your distribution channels, and your customers. But even with all the intuition in the world, marketers are still nervous. You never know how successful a program will be until it's over.

Good marketers are people with open minds and good senses of intuition. Most of all, they know how to look at information, check into what's going on, and get a feel for what's happening in the market. Interestingly enough, many people in marketing are former salespeople with five to ten years of sales experience. But usually they were not the top salespeople. Top salespeople are often cocky, self-confident, dominating, and seldom uncertain about their ability to sell anything. Top salespeople are usually lousy marketers. People who have doubts and wonder what's happening and why are much more likely to be good marketers.

As you read on, keep in mind that marketing is an intuitive art. Your knowledge of your product or service is the key. If sections of this book inspire you to think of other areas that are important to your business, don't be afraid to list them and consider them as possible problems, opportunities, or marketing strategies.

PART 1

ANALYZING YOUR BUSINESS FROM A MARKETING PERSPECTIVE

The first marketing planning step in most books or articles on the subject is an evaluation of the current market situation. For example, a pharmacist might feel she is not getting enough traffic in her drugstore, that her HMO patient ratio is too high, and that she is not generating enough business in her gift shop.

She can't write an effective marketing plan if she only evaluates her current situation. Instead, she needs to first thoroughly understand her market. What is really important to the pharmacist is why traffic is slow. Once the pharmacist knows that, she will know how to improve traffic. This thorough analysis is also important for a successful company. It needs to know what it is doing well and what its future problems or opportunities could be.

Chapters 2–5 show how to analyze your customers, products, and distribution to understand what factors are important for your product or service. Chapter 6 deals with evaluating your current situation. At this point, you should be able to determine not only what your problems are, but why they exist.

As you go through the analysis, you should have two goals: (1) determining what factors control your marketing success and (2) determining what aspects of your business the marketing plan should address. As you read each section in Chapters 2–6, keep a list of the factors you feel are key marketing elements for your business.

The next five chapters cover a wide variety of topics. Some may not be applicable to your business. I recommend you read the entire chapter and avoid the temptation to skim over topics that don't pertain specifically to your business. The chapters are designed to help you start thinking about your business from a marketing perspective. A comment on a seemingly unrelated topic may lead you to think of a problem or opportunity in your business.

In Chapter 1, I emphasized that marketing is intuitive. Don't interpret that to mean that snap decisions are OK. What intuition indicates instead is that most marketing decisions will not have a clear-cut best strategy. The more you understand about your business, the better chance you have of discovering the right marketing moves.

CHAPTER 2

YOUR CUSTOMERS—WHO THEY ARE, WHY THEY BUY, AND WHAT THEY THINK OF YOUR PRODUCT

In Business magazine (April 1988, pages 41–44) ran a feature story on The Enhancery, a jewelry store in San Diego. The store's motto is, "Never say never to a customer." The Enhancery will get or do whatever the customer wants. The owners feel that "management by customer feedback" is the key to the store's success.

I've read hundreds of similar stories that emphasize that success comes from catering to the customer. Without a doubt, your relationship with customers is crucial, but few companies have the resources to do everything every customer wants. A company needs to focus on a few things the customer wants that the company can do well.

Another problem with simply listening to customers is that they may not tell you everything you need to know. Apple Computer's founders were convinced that they could sell personal computers. Customers didn't tell Apple that—customers had never thought of personal computers. A study of potential customers indicated that the market was ready.

To do successful marketing, you must understand the interaction between your customer and your product, but your analysis needs to go further than just what the customer tells you. Chapter 2 will guide you in this evaluation. Customers have at least one trait that makes analyzing them difficult—they look at a product and then think they decide whether they want to buy it or not based on few features. For example, someone in my office bought a Camaro. Why? He said he liked the Camaro's image. But in fact, he didn't just consider image. Instead, he had five to ten core features the car had to have before he would even consider buying it.

For instance, he would only buy an American car and he wanted a V6 engine, bucket seats, a high resale value, and space to travel with his two dogs. His final selection was based on image, but that selection was made from two or three cars that had his core features.

I pointed out to the person the core features that influenced his decision, and he agreed that they were important in his purchase decision. But he still says he bought the Camaro because of its image. The moral of this story: Don't take the customer's word at face value, and don't jump to any quick conclusions about why the customer really buys.

FEAR OF LOSS

When people do a customer analysis, they have a tendency to think only about the positive impact a product's features and benefits have on customers. But that is often less than half the story. The selling tactics of one of the most successful salespeople I've known were formulated on his theory that "fear of loss is a much greater motivator than opportunity for gain."

A good example of this was my marketing team's selection of a market research consultant. One firm's pitch was that its findings could increase our sales 25 to 100 percent. Another firm told us that in over 25 percent of its studies, it recommended canceling a product's introduction. We went with the second company.

Marketers don't like to talk about fear of loss marketing because it has the negative image of being very manipulative. Designer jeans are certainly an example of manipulative marketing using fear of loss. The reason some people pay double the price of an ordinary pair of jeans is that they are afraid that without designer jeans they will look out of step with the latest fashions.

Fear of loss goes far beyond that narrow definition. Every time a person considers buying your product, he or she evaluates not only what can be gained, but also what can be lost by the purchase. You must understand what aspects of your product will be negatively perceived. One negative feature can cancel out five to ten positive features. I talked to someone just home from a cruise who will never board that ship again because its restaurant had tattered menus. The state of the menu convinced the person that the ship owners did everything possible to cut costs. As you read this chapter, think of issues that either positively or negatively influence your customers.

WHO IS YOUR CUSTOMER?

It sounds like a simple question, but it rarely has a simple answer. I worked for a dental company for five years, and the marketing and sales departments never came to a consensus on who the customer was. Some people thought the customer was the dealer network through which the company sold. Others were convinced the customer was the dentist who eventually purchased the company's product. Both sides were right.

About half the dentists trusted the company's dealers and based purchase decisions largely on a dealer's recommendation. The other dentists went to trade shows, talked to other dentists, and made their own decisions.

Both sides at the dental company felt that the customer was the person who determined which products were purchased—not the person who paid the bill. Your customer is anyone who has a significant influence on the purchase decision.

As another example, consider a cardiologist. Are his customers his patients? Or are his customers the MDs who refer patients to him? Or is the customer the hospital with which the cardiologist wants to be affiliated? All three can be the customer, depending on the cardiologist's situation. If you are selling gourmet frozen food, is the customer the consumer or the grocer who can give the product premium shelf space? Again, the answer is both are customers.

When defining your customer, think first in broad terms. For example, a manufacturer selling fancy blouses might have a broad customer category of teenagers and women under 30. Then think in more specific terms, such as affluent teenagers. You want to understand your current customers in order to increase market share. But you also want to understand the broader market so that you can know the limitations of your marketing strategy and discover methods to expand sales.

For example, gourmet coffee sells for about $6.50 a pound, which is expensive for coffee. A small percentage of coffee drinkers, perhaps 5 percent, are willing to pay the premium price for gourmet coffee. A company's strategy of selling only gourmet coffee will always have the limitation of appealing to only 5 percent of coffee drinkers. If the company wants to rapidly expand sales, it might introduce a second brand of coffee at $3.50 a pound to appeal to a larger customer base.

If you sell to another business, you might describe customers as nursing homes, electronics manufacturers, or automotive suppliers. You might even break out customers as a segment of an industry, such as automotive finishers. But remember that companies don't buy products, people do. In business-to-business marketing, there are at least two customers: an industry and the person who makes the purchase decision.

Consider a consulting firm selling testing services that determine who will be an effective salesperson. As a rule the customers are high-technology companies with 15 or more salespeople. The consulting firm's first customers are high-technology industries. The consultants sell their program to sales managers. The consultants' second customers are sales managers. The consultants' marketing approach must address the needs of both high-technology companies and sales managers.

Capital equipment sales can be even more complicated. First, you must convince manufacturing engineers that a product meets the needs of their production process. The engineers then put through a capital authorization request that the accountants and top management must approve. In effect, you not only have to market to engineers, but then you need to turn the engineers into salespeople to sell the product to top management.

When deciding who your customer is, think beyond the obvious. Everyone who can have a strong influence on the purchase decision is someone you should consider a customer. One last example of looking beyond the obvious is microprocessor manufacturers (the semiconductor building blocks of computers). Microprocessor manufacturers believe that software designers are customers even though they may purchase few microprocessors. A microprocessor won't be useful for most applications unless software designers develop software that fits it. Microprocessor manufacturers realize that their market expands with every piece of software developed for their product. So even though software companies may buy few microprocessors, they are key customers.

Government agencies are an example of what can happen when you don't know who a customer is. A farm state set up an agency to retrain displaced farmers. The agency surveyed the market and felt welding would be a good skill to offer. Welding also appealed to the farmers. But the agency's efforts never had a significant impact on unemployment.

What happened? The agency put all its efforts into who it felt were its customers—the displaced farmers. But the agency's real customers were the businesses that would eventually hire the farmers.

Even though welding was a job skill in demand, it represented only 5 to 10 percent of the available jobs. The agency would have been better off setting up on-the-job training programs with businesses. At the very least, the agency needed to get businesses more involved with the program.

WHAT'S YOUR CUSTOMER PROFILE?

Once you've determined who your customers are, you should profile them in two ways:

1. Actual customers versus desired customers
2. Competitors' customers and their profiles

Your customer profile should contain items such as age, income, geographic location, and so on. Anything that you feel is significant about your customers should be listed.

For example, a deli owner needs to know what type of customer she is attracting versus the type of customer she needs to succeed. The deli owner may find that she is selling primarily to teenagers from a local high school, but the teenagers only spend $1 or $2 per visit. The deli owner really wants to get more family trade, which averages $12 to $15 per visit.

A more detailed example is George's Tire and Auto Center. It's located in a middle-class, suburban neighborhood that has several office complexes. George decided on this location because five of the ten local gas stations had dropped their service bays. George felt his customers would be car owners who lived or worked within a three-mile radius of his business.

The store opened, offering prices 10 percent below its two main competitors. After nine months, the business was breaking even. George was concerned though because sales had flattened out in the last three months. A customer profile revealed that 85 percent of the store's customers were from a 1/3-mile radius of the store. Before opening his business, George had talked to his competitors, who had given him the impression that they were drawing customers from a three-mile radius. This radius was confirmed by one of George's mechanics who had worked for a competitor. George investigated why he was getting customers from a smaller area than his competitors. It turned out that one competitor had a shuttle bus while the other had two well-regarded mechanics.

George started drawing customers from within a wider radius after he added his own shuttle service and hired a mechanic who specialized in foreign cars.

Don't forget to profile all of your customers. Consider the gourmet frozen food company discussed earlier. The company has two customers: the consumer and the stores that stock the gourmet products. The company might find that 90 percent of its consumer customers are affluent and 10 percent middle class. The gourmet food company might profile the stores that carry its products as 40 percent gourmet deli shops and 60 percent upscale grocery stores.

HOW LOYAL ARE YOUR CUSTOMERS?

Customer loyalty is a barometer of how effective a marketing strategy is. If a marketing program is an effective strategy, customers will demonstrate loyalty. But how much loyalty should you expect? There are four rules regarding the nature of the product or service that determine the degree of loyalty you can expect.

People visit grocery stores frequently, and the stores tend to develop a loyal customer base. However, people use other businesses (such as appliance stores) rarely, and those stores tend not to have loyal customers. The first rule on loyalty, therefore, is that a product purchased frequently will have higher customer loyalty than a product purchased infrequently.

The second rule is that the more differentiated a product is from its competitors, the more likely it is to have a loyal customer following. Dr Pepper, for instance, is a unique-tasting soft drink with a loyal customer base.

People offering professional services, such as doctors, lawyers, dentists, and so on, also tend to have relatively loyal customers. The trait that determines loyalty for professionals is how well informed the customer is. Generally customers don't know much about the services being offered. Therefore, once a customer finds a professional she or he can trust, the customer tends to be loyal. The third rule is that the more well informed a customer is, the less likely he or she is to be loyal.

The fourth rule on customer loyalty is that companies targeting a broad market, such as General Motors, will have lower customer loyalty than a company targeting a smaller niche market, such as Audi.

Try and judge your customer loyalty based on these four rules. Also look at your competitors and see how they measure up. Typically the company with the highest degree of customer loyalty will be more profitable and have a better chance for long-term success than its competitors. Always look for ways to improve your customer loyalty.

An understanding of how much loyalty customers have toward your type of product is important to the thrust of your marketing programs. If you are in a business with a loyal customer base, you may want to concentrate your resources on marketing tactics that give results over the long term, such as image ads. Soft drink ads are an example of image advertising. If customers are not loyal in your market, you probably need marketing tactics with short-run results. Examples of short-run programs are rebate offers, price discounts, and giveaway prizes. Make sure that your product's marketing tactics are appropriate for the type of loyalty your customers exhibit.

HOW DOES THE CUSTOMER DECIDE TO BUY?

Marketing requires you to keep digging until you find all the information needed to develop a sound strategy. Tracking the path of a customer's buying decision is one area where digging is particularly important.

Joan is a typical consumer who is going to purchase a microwave oven. Here are the steps she takes in making her decision:

Step 1: Joan starts to think that maybe she should buy a microwave oven.

Step 2: On a casual basis, Joan talks to friends, watches ads, and reads magazines with information about microwaves. She does this over a six- to nine-month period.

Step 3: Joan leans toward two or three brands of microwaves.

Step 4: Joan looks more critically at the two or three brands she has chosen. She also starts to decide on the features that are most important to her.

Step 5: Joan enters an appliance store with an idea of what she wants. Joan is ready to buy.

Step 6: Even though Joan is ready to buy, she still needs reassurance that she is making the right choice. She talks to a salesperson who explains which features are available on each microwave. The salesperson might at this time try to switch Joan to a brand she had not intended to buy.

> Depending on how much assurance Joan needs, she may buy a product she hadn't considered initially.

Understanding how your customer decides to buy gives key marketing information. It tells you where to focus resources, whether in the early phases of the buying decision, or at the point of purchase, or both. In the case of the microwave, where a company should concentrate its resources depends on how thoroughly it can convince Joan that its microwave is the best choice before she walks into the store. If the company can't convince Joan in advance that it has the best microwave, it should concentrate its resources on the point of sale.

Tracking the buying decision also points out where to focus your long-term strategy. In the microwave example, it's clear that the manufacturers need to focus on differentiating their products so retail outlets can't switch customers to an alternate brand.

How Safe Does the Customer Feel When Buying Your Product?

In most buying decisions, how safe the customer feels is one of the two or three most important marketing points to consider. One of my favorite examples is the adage "No one ever got fired for buying an IBM computer." An IBM computer was the safe choice. On the other hand, a competitive computer may have been a better choice, but it would leave the buyer open to criticism. Customers do not want to take a chance on buying the wrong product.

Quaker Oats is an example of keeping an old, safe product the same. Quaker Oats has even kept the original oatmeal container.

If your product is not the obvious, safe choice, evaluate whether your marketing programs are addressing this problem. There are several tactics you might want to use. First, you could go after a small market where there aren't any competitors the customers consider safe. Going back to the IBM example, Apple, Digital, and Cray have all succeeded by going after a market where IBM wasn't the safe choice. Apple went after the school market, Digital concentrated on the engineering market, and Cray targeted the supercomputer market.

Another tactic that's useful when customers don't consider you the safe choice is to ally yourself with another organization. Young physicians might join an HMO or establish their offices in a prestigious medical building. Or, if you are a small retailer, you might want to give out coupons through a successful larger store; supermarket receipts often have coupons on the back from small retailers. Another example is an insurance company that sells its policies through an established brokerage house like Merrill Lynch.

Another tactic is to offer assurance about your product through money-back guarantees or extended warranties. Another is to build trust through personal associations. Young lawyers, accountants, and stockbrokers traditionally join the Chamber of Commerce, the Jaycees, country clubs, and other organizations. The resulting person-to-person contact with potential clients helps young professionals seem like safe choices.

Extra technical service is another way to give more assurance to the customer. I know of one company that gave every salesperson a truckload of spare parts. Customers were confident they would get good service from this company.

One tactic commonly used when a product is not the safe choice is dropping prices. I disapprove of this tactic. For example, currently many companies are introducing imitations of popular perfumes. The imitators are priced 40 to 70 percent lower than the authentic perfumes. But how many people buy them? Very few. Customers need assurance on products they don't fully understand. To offer a product at a lower price only adds to customer apprehension.

One argument I frequently hear is that Japanese companies often capture market share because of their low prices; therefore, the argument goes, dropping prices must be an effective strategy.

Japanese companies' low-price strategy does help them capture market share, but they also take positive steps to help assure customers that it is safe to purchase a Japanese product. Consider some of the markets Japanese companies have entered:

- Consumer electronics. The Japanese companies make better-quality products than American companies.
- Automobiles. The Japanese again offer higher-quality products than American companies.
- Personal computers. The Japanese waited to enter this market until personal computers had proven to be a useful tool. Then the Japanese produced IBM clones, taking advantage of IBM's reputation.

The Japanese companies' success in penetrating the U.S. market is due to the fact that they found a way to give customers assurance that their products are a safe choice *and* because they have lower prices.

In some cases you can't make your customers feel safe when buying your product. You may have a new product or be introducing a new technology. Your customers will buy because the products are innovative, creative, and daring. Play upon these emotions and minimize safety issues when selling truly innovative products.

WHAT DO YOUR CUSTOMERS WANT?

Determining what your customers want is a two-step process. First you break a market into segments; then you determine what customers in those segments want.

For example, a car company can't really define what a car buyer wants because car customers buy for too many diverse reasons. Some customers buy the cheapest car available while others buy the most expensive. To overcome the wide variety of customer needs, the car company first divides customers into various segments, such as economy car buyers, low-cost sports car buyers, luxury car buyers, and so on. Then the car company picks a segment—for instance, low-cost sports car buyers—and determines what this customer wants.

The most common model used to break a market into segments is a matrix. As an example, I'll study a home builder. He might develop a matrix based on location versus price.

FIGURE 2–1
Market Segment Matrix for New Residential Construction

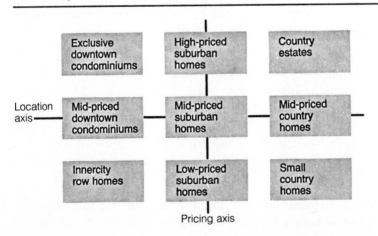

A builder might use this matrix to determine the next development project. He could survey customers in his geographic area and find out that 15 percent would like to live on a country estate. He could then survey area builders and see that country estates represent only 10 percent of new construction. The builder then knows that his next development could be country estates.

A way to increase the benefit from a matrix is to break out nine segments based on the two axes. Next to each segment, list its percentages of the market and its percentage of products available. I'll prepare this chart based on the same home builder.

FIGURE 2–2
Market Segment Matrix with Additional Information

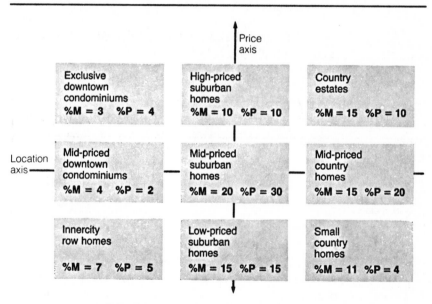

%M = the percentage of the market the segment comprises.
%P = the percentage of the products in the market that serves this segment.

This matrix gives the builder even more information about which market looks most attractive: the small country home market, because it has the biggest difference between percentage of the market (11 percent) and percentage of homes available (4 percent).

Three models can help you decide what customers want within a market segment. The first model tries to establish the importance of various features to the customer. I call it a compromise model. It is very useful in markets where no one can offer all the features customers want and charge a price they are willing to pay. Therefore, every manufacturer or business offers a different set of features for the customer to choose from. The steps involved in this model are:

1. List all the buying concerns of the customer.
2. Separate the list into three categories.
   a. Must have.
   b. Important to have.
   c. Nice to have.
3. Estimate the relative value on a scale of one to ten for each important and nice-to-have feature.

As an example, I'll use a builder who has elected to build mid-price suburban homes. His chart would look like this:

Feature	Relative Rating
Must Have	
Priced under $90,000	10
Three bedrooms	10
Good schools	10
1/4-acre lots	10
Important to Have	
Two baths	7
Four bedrooms	4
Easy commuting distance	8
Family room	5
Nice to Have	
Good playgrounds	3
Low taxes	3
Close to shopping	2
Nice view	2

This chart shows the builder what features could be added if he can't build within easy commuting distance. He might compensate by adding features such as two baths plus a nice view. From the chart, the builder knows that his homes must always be priced under $90,000. His marketing strategy needs to offer a mix of features that will appeal to the buyer at that price.

Another excellent feature of a compromise chart is that it helps you focus your marketing efforts on the features that are most important to the customer.

Other markets aren't governed by a compromise model, but instead use a reason-for-purchase model. For example, I buy paint from three different stores. The exterior of my house was painted with a Sears paint before I purchased it. I've always painted it the same color, primarily because I do not want to go through the trouble of painting it a new color. I always buy my ceiling paint from Sherwin Williams because I've had trouble in the past painting ceilings with other brands. The last store I buy paint at custom blends any color my wife or I want.

In a market like paint, it's handy to list the percentages of purchases by major reason. Paint manufacturers would have a chart like this:

29%	10%	8%	13%	8%	32%
Price	Brand loyalty	Same color	Customized color	Best paint	Purchase from favorite store

To a local paint store the chart would look like this:

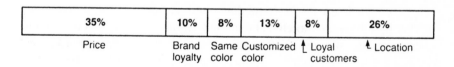

35%	10%	8%	13%	8%	26%
Price	Brand loyalty	Same color	Customized color	Loyal customers	Location

In other markets, products may not provide what the customer ultimately wants, but rather the product allows the customer to take a step toward achieving what he or she wants. Consider lawn fertilizer. Customers don't want lawn fertilizer—they want a beautiful lawn. If your product doesn't offer the customer what he or she wants, you can use an ultimate goal model. In this model you list every step needed to give customers their ultimate goal or what they want. I'll use a customer's ultimate goal of a beautiful lawn as an example.

FIGURE 2–3
Steps Required to Achieve a Beautiful Lawn

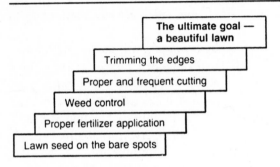

A fertilizer manufacturer tries to offer as many of the steps as possible. Weed-and-feed fertilizer and grass seed/fertilizer mixtures are two options that fertilizer manufacturers use, but they find it difficult to combine many of the steps. This has led to the popularity of lawn services, such as Chemlawn, who will do everything necessary to provide the customer with a beautiful lawn except for cutting and trimming.

All four models show that a customer buys for a wide variety of reasons. You must find a group of customers to target to be successful. I've never seen a marketing program yet that will appeal to every customer.

Look back on the four models, and decide if your product and marketing efforts are targeted at a market segment. If not, you must focus your marketing strategy. You should also look at your target market and decide if it's big enough to support your sales plans. If not, try to find another market segment that you can expand into in order to increase your potential customer base.

HOW WELL DO CUSTOMERS KNOW YOUR NAME?

Getting name recognition is important, but it can be difficult and expensive. You need some recognition if customers rarely need your services. Examples are H & R Block and a piano store. As an example of how this can affect a business, consider the two bicycle shops once in my area. One shop had been there for years and was well known. It also was junky looking and didn't have very good service. The other shop had great atmosphere and decor, good service, and an excellent inventory, but it put all its money in the store, and no one knew it was in business. The second store eventually failed.

One of the pitfalls of marketing is that you could spend all your time thinking about your own or your competitor's product and tend to forget that your customers rarely think about these products. That's why name recognition is so important. Most people think they can get this recognition fairly easily, but that's just not the case. In the shopping center near my house, for example, a party goods paper outlet recently had an unspectacular grand opening. When my wife had to buy some items for a party, she drove five miles to another store to get them. She forgot about the nearby store that she had driven past 100 times. I get sales flyers about products all the time, but when I want to buy something, unless I get a sales flyer just then, I go to the company I remember.

As a general rule, if you need name recognition, figure out how much you feel it is going to cost, and then spend $2^{1}/_{2}$ times that figure. This rule reflects how important name recognition is for some businesses, as well as how hard name recognition is to get. If you have a retail business, the sign and outward appearance of the shop also should be considered as an important way to establish name recognition.

WHAT DOES THE CUSTOMER THINK ABOUT YOUR PRODUCT?

The customer's perception of your product or company is crucial in determining its success. Never take customers for granted. Remember too that what the customer thinks of you is what you should consider to be your actual position. For example, if the customer feels you have second-rate products, then that's what you have. Remember, the customer has a much lower image of your product than the people who work with you, so it's important to get out and find out what your customers or potential customers really think of your product. Don't be surprised if you find that people have a narrow view of a store or product; this is typical. Take for example the lumber yards in my area. One yard is considered to have the best lumber but is expensive; another yard has inexpensive lumber but of very poor quality; the third yard has low prices but reasonable quality.

Customers have a short list of feelings about a product or store. In one sense, this is good because it identifies a specific area to correct. It can be confusing though because people will remember the one thing they like or dislike most. If you correct the one dislike that's strongest, you may find other problems that were never mentioned. Consider a discount department store with a reputation for slow checkout lines. A new manager might solve this problem only to find out customers think the store has shoddy merchandise. On the other hand, if people have a favorable impression of you for one reason, take great care to promote and protect that impression.

While customers will have a limited overall impression of your product, service, or store, there are specific areas you should study. They are:

- *Customer Service.* Customers want good service and will pay for it. This is an easy area in which to be better than the competition if only because so many companies have poor customer service. Make your customers feel good, and they will come back. You only have to think about your own experiences to see how poor service can affect people. The major difficulty in getting good customer service is that it requires a positive attitude among employees, which can be difficult to attain.
- *Innovativeness of Products.* How innovative are your products or, in the case of a store, your merchandise? Customers like to be associated with the leader in technology. This image for your firm, either good or bad, is something that can take years to change, so react quickly to any negative customer impressions.
- *Quality of Products.* Given a choice, I'd rather market a high-priced, high-quality product. People want quality and, for the most part, are willing to pay for it. Nothing else will keep people buying and recommending your product the way good quality will; and nothing will stop people from buying your product the way poor quality will. However, it is not always the true quality that counts, but what people perceive the quality to be. I've always marveled at how some manufacturers put one or two cheap-looking parts on an expensive item. This gives the whole product the image of poor quality and is why fit, finish, and trim items require meticulous attention.

If customers feel you have high-quality products, promote that vigorously. If customers feel your quality is poor, you've got serious problems. Sometimes it is even easier to introduce a new product rather than try to change a poor-quality image. If your product quality is low, evaluate seriously if it is worth promoting the product at all.

One thing you never want to do is to promote the quality of your product when you don't really have it. Remember to always consider your customers to be knowledgeable; they will have a good idea of your quality, and you won't fool them. For instance, all the hype over automobile manufacturers' six- or seven-year warranty is nonsense. I don't know anyone who thinks a car with a two-year warranty has lower quality than a car with a seven-year warranty.

- *Price and Price/Value Relationship.* These are fairly self-explanatory. Don't be afraid if customers think you are high-priced as long as your price/value relationship is in line. And if your price/value is not what it should be, think first of adding value rather than lowering the price. Often people associate quality, in part, with price. I remember never trying a Comfort Inn Motel because I associated low price with poor quality. It is also difficult to raise your price without damaging your price/value relationship. Once people get used to your product or service at a certain price, they won't think it has good value at a higher price.

WHY DO CUSTOMERS BUY FROM YOU?

Are your customers buying from you because of product features, brand name loyalty, location, product popularity, a superior salesforce, marketing campaigns, price, compatibility with other products, customer service, superior inventory, or another reason? If you find you can't get a handle on why people buy from you, if it seems people just wander in or buy by accident, you probably have a problem. It is important, from a marketing point of view, to know the reason or reasons that people buy from you. Without that, it's difficult to really have a strong, positive identity.

There are many examples of how understanding your customers' motives can benefit you. My neighborhood hardware store realizes people shop there because of convenience. It has virtually every hardware product jammed into the store, plus it always has three or four clerks present to help customers. The only mistake it makes is not charging enough of a price premium.

People buy Coke because of its great tradition. That's why changing to new Coke was a bad marketing decision. In the car industry, people pay, to a large degree, for the image created by a car. Don't be overly concerned if you don't have an impressive reason for people to buy your product. As I mentioned before, customers often associate only one or two impressions with each company. Friendly service or a large inventory can be sufficient buying motivation for your customers.

WHY DON'T PEOPLE BUY FROM YOU?

There are many prospective customers who could buy a product but don't. Figuring out why these people don't buy from you can be helpful. Of course, there are many reasons, but what you are looking for is a trend that gives you clues on how your business can be improved. This information can be difficult to obtain. Large companies sometimes hire an outside market research firm to find out why people don't buy from them. If that's impractical, pay close attention to what your salesforce says about why it loses sales, and try to interview people who stop buying from you. In a retail business, ask family and friends to listen for ad-lib remarks they might hear. Remember that bad news is important to know. Often it's more important to know than good news.

SUMMARY

When evaluating marketing problems, it is crucial to consider the entire marketing situation before making a decision. Otherwise, you can make mistakes. Since I mentioned Coke earlier, I'll consider its situation. Sales had been slowly declining, and Coke was losing market share. Coke's customers were switching to another product because they liked a sweeter-tasting soft drink. The traditional method of making up for lost sales is to introduce new products such as Cherry Coke in this case. But in the soft drink market, tremendous promotion is necessary to obtain even a small market share. This is not an easy problem to handle. What

Coke needed was a sweet-tasting soft drink to compete with Pepsi. It also needed the product to take a 4 to 8 percent market share so the company could afford to market it. Pepsi would never give up that large a share. We can sympathize with the decision made by Coke's executives, but they went wrong when they didn't evaluate their customers carefully enough.

Before moving on, list the five most important traits of your customers. Then list the five things you do best and the five things you do worst toward meeting their needs. Don't make a snap judgment yet about your marketing objectives, but keep these points in mind as you read the next four chapters.

CHAPTER 3

YOUR PRODUCT—WHAT ARE YOU OFFERING?

I've had many people tell me that a well-designed marketing program will sell anything. I don't agree. A marketing program might get a product off to a fast start, but the product won't sustain that momentum unless the product meets customer needs. For example, the Pontiac Fiero was introduced in 1984 with a lot of fanfare and a sound marketing program. The Fiero sold well for two years, but now it's being discontinued.

What happened? Pontiac's market research found a demand for a two-seat sports car, and customers responded favorably when the Fiero, positioned as a low-priced, two-seat sports car, was introduced. But the Fiero had a sports car body built over what was originally meant to be a small commuter car. The Fiero lacked the power and maneuverability that sports car buyers wanted.

A bad marketing program, on the other hand, will kill a well-designed product. Marketing's definition calls for creating a link between a product and its customers. For a product to be successful, a marketing program must start the linking process. A marketing program must make the customer aware of the product, show why the customer needs the product, and then put the product where the customer can buy it.

Before continuing, I should define what I mean by a product. A product is the total package of goods and services that is offered to a customer. For example, a retail store's product includes its merchandise, in-store layout, merchandising racks, customer return policies, checkout clerks, in-store promotional material, and anything else in the store that might impact on a customer.

Remember as you read this chapter that customers are knowledgeable and intelligent, and you must avoid underestimating them. The reason I mention this here is that you will be evaluating how well marketing programs fit a product. People typically overestimate the value of their products and marketing programs, while downplaying the value of competitors' products and programs. The customer will be making an intelligent, objective evaluation. You need to do the same to develop a strong marketing program.

As you read the chapter, look for key marketing elements of your business that you might focus on. The chapter is broken down into five sections:

1. Understanding the product.
2. How the product is positioned.
3. The product's strengths and weaknesses.
4. Pricing policy.
5. How to add value to a product.

Again, keep a list of important marketing elements that you will want to consider using in the marketing plan.

UNDERSTANDING THE PRODUCT

What Type of Business Are You In?

Answer this question by describing your business as more than just a retail, service, or manufacturing business.

Consider gas stations. Some stations are still the traditional full-service stations; they are in the business of taking care of your car. Other stations have just an express island and are in the business of selling gas. Some gas stations offer sodas, beer, and a few other items; they are in the business of providing everything someone needs when stopping for gas on a trip. Other stations are really full-service convenience stores.

Another example is manufacturers who sell test equipment. One manufacturer may have one product for measurement that the company will sell to any industry. This company's customers might have to buy equipment from other suppliers to complete a measurement system. Another manufacturer might sell total measurement systems, including the test product the first company sells. Still another manufacturer might sell a measurement system designed for only one industry.

Once you have decided what business you are in, decide if this is the business you want. For example, if you are product oriented, selling only one product, you may decide you want to be in the systems business. You also should evaluate how close your actual business is to your desired business. For example, if you are in the business of selling test systems and you only provide 90% of the equipment required, you've found a major problem area.

Often businesses get settled in their operation without realizing they're not doing everything necessary for their business. An example is the American car industry. General Motors, Ford, and Chrysler are in the business of supplying cars for the entire population. In the late 1970s and early 1980s, car manufacturers moved to simplify manufacturing. The result was that their upscale cars became variations of their mid-range cars. That didn't satisfy the public's desire for a highly differentiated car as a status symbol. The result is that now Audis, Saabs, BMWs, and others have significant sales in this profitable market formerly dominated by Buicks, Oldsmobiles, and Mercurys.

Describe Your Product

Describe your product in less than ten words from your customers' viewpoint. Some examples: You sell the premium blender on the market. Your store has the best-quality lumber; your product has the lowest price; United is the largest airline in the country; Northwest Airlines has the best flights to Minneapolis; you sell traditional furniture. Customers won't think of your product in any more detail than these examples.

HOW IS YOUR PRODUCT POSITIONED?

Positioning is usually defined as targeting a market segment or niche and then developing a product and a promotional campaign to appeal to that segment. I also believe that positioning should include differentiating a product from the competition's. For example, Hyundai's positioning strategy is to offer a dependable car for under $6,000. Hyundai's strategy includes the following key positioning elements:

Hyundai targeted the economy car market.

Hyundai's features of low cost and dependability are important to economy car buyers.

Hyundai is the only dependable car available that costs less than $6,000.

Is Your Strategy Focused?

Failure to focus a product on a market segment is a major cause of business failure. Roy Rogers fast-food outlets are an example. Roy Rogers sells fried chicken, hamburgers, and roast beef sandwiches, and has a salad bar. I'm not sure what market Roy Rogers has targeted. A Roy Rogers outlet by my home just closed, which indicates how Roy Rogers' profit performance lags behind the industry average.

As an example of a well-focused plan, consider a carpenter in my neighborhood who does home repairs and remodeling. He has at least 15 competitors, but the carpenter has been successful because he has concentrated on homes within a 10-square-block area. The carpenter knows the homes in the development, and the residents of the development know him.

When building repairs slowed down in the carpenter's target area, he went after another small market about three miles away. Again, the carpenter concentrated his efforts.

Two lawyers who left the public defender's office in northern New Jersey provide an interesting study of the value of targeting a market. One lawyer decided to specialize in environmental law. He started his private practice but initially had trouble attracting clients. To make enough income, the lawyer worked part time for the public defender's office. In his private practice, he continued to refuse clients who didn't need help on environmental issues.

The second lawyer started his practice by taking any and all clients. For the first two years, his practice was busier than the environmentalist's. But after the first two years, the lawyers' positions reversed as the environmental practice grew rapidly.

I must emphasize the need for a critical evaluation of your market segment focus. Numerous times I've heard people say they are concentrating on a specific market segment, but I've found that their ads, products, brochures, and other marketing efforts did not indicate this. The reason people usually cite for not gearing their marketing efforts to a particular segment is that they don't want to miss any potential customers. Most people have trouble believing that the highest sales volume is generated by concentrating on a small percentage of the market. Don't try to have a product that can be sold to every customer.

How Is Your Product Differentiated?

A marketer is responsible for differentiating a product from competitors' products. If a product is similar to a competitor's product, a marketer needs to use tactics to change the product in order to differentiate it. The marketer may use better product warranties, more efficient customer service, quicker delivery, or more favorable terms.

Sometimes the word *positioning* is substituted for the term *differentiation*. I like to make a distinction between the two because the word *positioning* is overworked. I went to a mall recently and noticed five clothing stores geared toward teenagers and young adults. Two names you might recognize are The Gap and The Limited. All five stores carried jeans and casual sportswear. None of these stores did a good job of differentiation. They had a clear target market, a well-focused ad program, and merchandise that supported their image, but the problem was that all five stores were almost exactly alike. I even made two visits to each store to see if I had missed something. The stores had a good positioning strategy, but very poor product differentiation.

This is by no means an uncommon situation. I've heard people explain how well their product was positioned, but they didn't understand that there are three distinct steps to positioning:

1. Position the product so that it serves a particular market segment. This is typically done by a company before a product's introduction.
2. Position the product so targeted customers feel the product meets their needs. This is usually done with an ad or other promotional campaigns.
3. Position the product as being different than competitors' products. This should be done both in the product planning and promotional planning stages.

I recently completed a study on electronic assembly equipment that showed me just how marketers can lose track of product differentiation. I was interested in assembly equipment that would meet the demands of short production runs. I received brochures from 15 companies. What I found was:

Every company said that its product was ideal for short production runs. They all had a well-defined target market.

Every company listed its benefits that pertained to short production runs. In this example, the main benefits were fast component placement times and flexible design that handled a wide variety of electronic components.

Not one brochure told the reader how a product was different from the competitors'. I had to study detailed diagrams of product features and lengthy specification sheets to figure out how the products differed.

What really surprised me was that the products actually had many differences. Some companies placed a premium on speed while others worried about accuracy. No two companies had the same package of features, but the companies made me work hard to realize that.

You should also consider your competitors. Does one competitor have its product better differentiated that you do? If so, you need to change your product, so it is just as differentiated. The push here, usually from your salesforce and management, will be to try to be just like your competition (especially if they are successful). Resist this temptation, and instead figure out how you can have another, just as advantageous differentiation. Again, don't base your product changes on what *you* think the product's differentiation is, but rather on what your *customers* perceive to be the differentiation. If customers don't think you have some way of distinguishing yourself, then you are not differentiated.

What "Romance" Is Involved in Your Products?

No matter what the product is, there is a substantial amount of emotion involved in any buying decision. Therefore, an important consideration is the romance, status, or style of a product. A vacation to the Caribbean has romance. A new Corvette has status. A new $300 suit has style. If your product or service involves romance, status, or style, you should position it with that in mind. Don't try features and benefits positioning strategies.

One thing that is important to remember in marketing is that some people are image conscious while others are not. Image-conscious people like ads and marketing programs that have image appeal. People who are not image conscious like features or benefits ads. If you have a product with romance or a product for image-conscious customers, make sure your marketing program is appropriate.

How Important Is Change?

There are two types of product change that a company may need to introduce. The first is small product changes that don't alter a product's performance. For example, a singles bar may change its decor every three years, or a toaster may change its color scheme. Some products, especially consumer products like clothing, require frequent product changes.

The second type of change is significant technological change. High-technology companies constantly need to introduce new products to avoid having their products labeled outdated. Semiconductors are an example. Fairchild was one of the first technology industry giants, but did not change its technology fast enough, and the company ended up being purchased by a competitor.

Sometimes market position is important in determining the need for change. For example, Ivory soap has been a market leader for 50 years, and therefore the company does not change the product. Soaps introduced more recently might benefit from a constant stream of product changes.

Service businesses have some unique marketing problems. New competitors can often easily enter a market and imitate a service company's product. Service companies typically counter this by emphasizing their reliability. Service companies often overlook the marketing benefits of changing their product, especially when the changes are at a customer's request. A janitorial service company, for example, constantly asked its customers what other services it could provide. One customer asked the company if it would change light bulbs. The result for the janitorial company was not only a little more business, but a loyal customer besides.

Where Is Your Product in Its Life Cycle?

Different types of people buy a product during the various phases of its life cycle. For instance, when you first introduce a product, don't talk about money-back guarantees or features and benefits. The customers

FIGURE 3–1
Product Life Cycle Curve

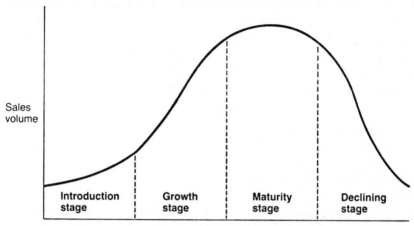

Sales
volume

| Introduction | Growth | Maturity | Declining |
| stage | stage | stage | stage |

Time a product is on the market

who buy new products are innovators. They want to see the words "new," "innovative," "breakthrough," and "technological advancement" in product literature. The compact disc's introduction followed this tact. The entire positioning strategy has been that the new technology of compact discs sounds better than records.

The next market phase, rapid growth, occurs when a product concept has been accepted by customers as useful. When a product is in its rapid growth stage, marketing efforts should concentrate on getting the product into the market where customers can buy it. When compact discs were first introduced in Philadelphia, they were sold only in music and a few department stores. When compact discs entered the growth phase of the market, they were sold everywhere: stereo stores, appliance stores, department stores, and catalog showrooms.

In the third phase, maturity, sales volumes level off, and marketers need to start differentiating products to maintain sales growth. For example, TVs are in their maturity stage, and manufacturers offer oversized TV screens, TVs with higher resolution, TVs that are cable ready, TVs that are low priced, TVs that have every possible electronic gadget, and so on.

The fourth phase, decline, occurs when a new product concept comes onto the market and displaces the old one. As an example, traditional department stores have entered their declining market phase.

The concept of a big store with a wide variety of products has been displaced by suburban malls with a variety of retail stores all under one roof. The way for a department store to survive the declining phase of its life cycle is to change its product. Sears has changed to the "Sears Store of the Future" with an entirely different store layout and with each merchandising rack clearly detailing the features of the product. Sears also offers a host of other features, such as Dean Witter financial centers, optical departments, and photography studios. Bloomingdale's counters its declining market cycle by creating a destination store that is fun to visit because of its exotic merchandise.

A department store that didn't change was Gimble's. It lost a lot of money before selling out to Stern's, which is making the same mistakes.

Is Your Product Revolutionary?

If you have a revolutionary product, you probably will find that customers are reluctant to accept the product's radical differentiation. There are three tactics you might be using to overcome buyer reluctance to such a product. The first is to move the market to your concept in stages. Ford did this before introducing the Taurus and Sable models' dramatically different aerodynamic look. Two years prior to the Taurus's introduction, Ford started advertising aerodynamics on Thunderbirds, educating the market on the importance of rounded, aerodynamic lines.

The second tactic for introducing revolutionary products is an aggressive public relations campaign. People who purchase new products are innovators, people who are willing to take chances. To get innovators interested in a new product, typically you only need to let them know a product is on the market. An aggressive public relations campaign (placing articles in newspapers, trade journals, and so on) is often enough. A public relations campaign has the additional advantage of enhancing a product's image. Customers are more willing to believe a story in a magazine or newspaper than they are to believe a company's ads and literature. The first two tactics work best when the product is an important purchase to the customer.

A third tactic to use when a product is revolutionary is to run a promotion campaign with high visibility. When Miller Lite was introduced, it was a revolutionary product. Beer drinkers had always been portrayed as rugged individualists or "macho" men; and bringing out a low-calorie beer was definitely radical. Miller's tactic was to run an extensive ad campaign. Although Miller's excellent ads featured popular former athletes, Miller was successful because it inundated consumers with the message. An extensive promotion campaign usually works best with a low-risk purchase. If someone purchased Miller Lite and didn't like it, the purchase only cost the person a few dollars. Typically, customers like more assurance than an ad campaign can offer if the purchase is not low risk.

The personality of your customers is important when introducing a revolutionary product. For example, I introduced a test product to a new market where the product was unknown. I learned to prioritize potential customers by personality rather than by how much the customer needed the product. I found that unless a prospect wanted to look like a hero and was willing to take a chance, he or she just wouldn't buy our product because it was new.

You also should consider customers' personalities when projecting sales growth of a new product. I once reviewed a marketing plan for introducing a new product to farmers that projected 10 percent market penetration in the first year. That was an impossible goal—farmers are just too conservative. The plan called for a huge promotion budget, which was a mistake since most farmers won't buy a product until it is well established.

Is Your Product a Solution?

Selling solutions is a technique used in high-tech marketing that makes sense for every marketing program. High-tech marketers try to position their product as a solution to a customer need rather than positioning it with features and benefits. Evaluating whether or not a business is selling a solution is important and can often lead to successful marketing programs as well as being an effective method for determining what product changes can increase sales.

The term *solution* is sometimes confused with features and benefits. For example, a luncheon meat has low fat and sodium content—that's a feature of the product. This luncheon meat is healthy to eat—that's the benefit to the customer of a luncheon meat with low fat and sodium content. This luncheon meat allows the preparation of any easy-to-make, nutritional lunch—that's the solution the luncheon meat offers.

A solution meets a customer's need, which is why he or she buys a product. People buy luncheon meat because they need to eat lunch. Customers want to buy solutions. As a rule, every step taken toward making a product a solution increases sales.

Although the luncheon meat manufacturer could advertise its product as a solution, luncheon meat does not offer a complete solution for a nutritional lunch. Bread, fruit, and milk are also necessary. But if the luncheon meat manufacturer offered discount coupons for fruit on the package, the company would be taking an extra step toward offering the customer a complete solution.

It is important to realize that when customers buy a product, they buy it to accomplish something. I purchase wallpaper, for instance, to make a room look nice. A wallpaper manufacturer that lets me know what color paint goes best with the wallpaper is taking an extra step toward offering a solution. A home-decorating center might show a corner of a beautiful room. When it lists matching wallpaper, paint, tile, and curtain styles, it too is moving toward offering a solution.

Somehow over the past years, the marketing rule that "people buy benefits, not features" has evolved. I would agree that benefits are better than features, but why not contribute to what the customer really wants—a solution? Knowing what part your product plays in satisfying a customer's need is essential to successful marketing. This knowledge offers many clues as to how to improve your marketing programs. Yet, surprisingly, I talk to many people who don't even know what basic customer need their product ultimately meets. A person who markets industrial test equipment told me his product offered a solution of fewer rejects; but what his customers really wanted was low manufacturing cost and a superior product.

What solution does a clothing store offer? It can make people look good. I've always thought this was the reason catalog sales have done well. They offer a much better solution than a clothing store; they attractively display outfits on people rather than clothes on a rack. The better a clothing store can display total outfits, the more successful it will be.

You need to determine what solution your product is ultimately working toward and then decide if customers can easily see how your product meets their need. If a customer has trouble doing that, you need a new marketing approach. A low sales closing rate is a good indication that your customers don't see how a product satisfies their need. Also remember that a customer may not buy until he or she realizes a product or group of products is a solution. So just because you may have a large market share doesn't mean that customers realize your product is a solution. For instance, I've often thought of buying a home computer, but I've never seen an easy-to-use package that has convinced me a home computer would be a useful tool.

Once I traveled with a company's top salesperson one week and with one of the company's lower-ranked salespeople the next week. They both gave excellent sales presentations, and both knew the product well. Both were dealing with engineers who wanted to equip an assembly line. The company sold about 40 percent of the equipment needed. The top salesperson recommended a total system to the customers, including other companies' products. The other salesperson considered only the 40 percent of the assembly line that the company's products covered. He wasn't offering a complete solution.

What Is Your Selling Proposition?

Examples of selling propositions are: Buy Coke because it tastes great. Buy Pepsi because it beats Coke in taste tests and is the "taste of a new generation." Buy Sony products because of their high quality. Buy a Camaro because it has a sports car look. Buy an IBM computer because it offers extensive product support.

A proposition can be feature oriented: buy a Chevette and get good gas mileage. A proposition can be service oriented: buy from Sears because they will accept any return. Or a proposition can be image oriented: buy a BMW because it's the Yuppie car. The important point is that your product has a selling proposition and that it's compelling enough to induce customers to buy your product. If your selling proposition is not strong, develop a new one. Often a selling proposition is all that a customer will remember about a product. You want to be sure that your proposition is significant enough that the customer thinks it's worth remembering.

YOUR PRODUCT'S STRENGTHS AND WEAKNESSES

Strengths

List all the strengths of your product, then prioritize the importance of each strength in two categories: first, the strengths as you promote them, and second, the strengths as the customer perceives them. Often companies run promotions that tout features that are not the product's greatest strengths. For example, Genaurdi's supermarkets in Philadelphia are promoted as family-run, friendly stores, but all my neighbors who shop at Genaurdi's do so because they like the stores' layout. You want the product strengths that you promote to be the ones that are most important to your customers.

Other times a product might have a strength that is not being promoted that the customer doesn't realize. Arm & Hammer, for example, discovered that customers didn't know what a good job their baking soda did absorbing refrigerator odors. Arm & Hammer promoted that feature and significantly increased sales.

Most products have at least a few strengths that are different than competitive products. Consequently, customers buy from different companies similar products for different reasons. Consider two M.D.s, one 55 and the other 30, whose practices are both in the same medical complex. Their respective strengths in order of importance are:

55-Year-Old M.D.	*30-Year-Old M.D.*
Served as a family doctor for years.	Known as very friendly; he spends extra time with each patient.
Associated with the area's most prestigious hospital.	Offers flexible hours; open two nights per week and Saturday mornings.
Widely known in the community.	Writes medical column for local newspaper.
Offers comfortable office.	Appeals to some patients because of his youth.

This example has two similar products with significantly different strengths. Some people prefer the 55-year-old doctor while others prefer the 30-year-old. Each doctor needs to develop his marketing strategy around his strengths.

Weaknesses

In Chapter 2 I discussed how customers look at a product for both positive and negative features. Often it takes five or ten positive features to cancel out a negative feature. Most, if not all, products are imperfect. Every marketer has to deal with product weaknesses constantly; the key is to minimize the damage of a product's weaknesses.

Again, start by listing your product's weaknesses. Now check off weaknesses that every competitor has, and weaknesses that don't hurt you in your target market. Finally, you need to address the weaknesses that remain by either redefining the target market or by developing a marketing campaign to compensate for the weaknesses. Listed below is a weakness evaluation chart for the 30-year-old M.D.

30-Year-Old M.D. Weakness	Weakness all competitors have	Weakness not important to target market	Weakness that needs addressing
Practice is difficult to access due to traffic congestion.	✔		
M.D. is too youthful for some patients.		✔	
Examining room equipment is old.			✔
M.D. tends to run late against his appointment schedule.			✔
M.D. is not well known in the area.			✔

The doctor has three weaknesses he should address. The first, that his examining room equipment is old, could be addressed by redecorating the rooms to draw attention away from the equipment or by acquiring new equipment. The second weakness, running late for appointments, could be addressed by spreading appointments out a little more. And the third weakness, not being well known, could be addressed by the doctor joining more local community groups or organizing a health screening day.

The other two categories of weaknesses, weaknesses all competitors have and weaknesses not important to the target market, also provide possibilities for a marketing strategy. If a product or company can overcome weaknesses every competitor has, it might be able to create a meaningful, differentiated strategy. As an example, consider fast-food outlets. Nutrition experts always complain about the low nutritional content of fast foods. If a fast-food chain could develop a nutritious menu that people liked, it would have a terrific marketing advantage.

Sometimes a weakness that is not important to a target market prevents a product from expanding to new markets. If a company can solve that weakness, it might expand its market. For example, a specialty shop in a downtown area could specialize in clothes for the working executive woman. The store might have a weakness of being closed on Saturday and Sunday. That's not important to the target market of women working downtown, but if the store were to stay open on Saturdays, it might expand its market to include working women in the suburbs.

PRICING

Pricing is a volatile issue and is critical to a product's success. It is important not only because pricing affects profits, but also because pricing is important to a product's image.

As a rule, I'm reluctant to drop a price. Often there are better tactics available to a marketer to raise sales volume. Not that lowering prices is always poor strategy; sometimes it is effective. But for the most part, lowering prices is a vastly overused marketing tool.

Law of Supply and Demand

Every businessperson in the country at one time or another has heard about the law of supply and demand; numerous times I've been told a price decrease is justified because of this law. In some situations the law of supply and demand works. Certainly it holds true in personal computers and calculators; as their prices dropped, demand increased substantially. But much of the time, the law of supply and demand won't hold true.

The law of supply and demand applies:

When a significant price drop is possible. A significant price drop can dramatically increase market size. Personal computer and calculator prices dropped over 50 percent the first few years they were offered to the public.

When the product is a discretionary purchase. As prices fall, demand will go up. Soft drinks are a discretionary purchase.

When you have a small market share. A small competitor can drop its price and raise its sales volume without a larger competitor immediately following. For example, if a small local brewery dropped its beer prices $2 a case, its volume would go up. The big beer competitors would not want to drop their prices to protect a small market share.

The law of supply and demand won't apply:

When your market is saturated. Virtually everyone in the United States has one or more TVs. If TV manufacturers were to lower the price, the overall market size would stay the same.

When you have a leading market share position. Competitors can't afford to let a price decrease from a market leader go unanswered; the competitors stand to lose too much volume. When General Motors introduced rebates, Ford and Chrysler immediately followed. Sales went up for a short period, but now have leveled out at the sales level that would have existed without rebates.

When your product is necessary. Most people consider paper towels necessary around the home, but people can use only so many paper towels. If the price drops, people's purchases won't increase.

Take care in applying these guidelines. Even if the law of supply and demand applies, this doesn't mean that the increased volume will compensate for the loss in profit per unit sale. In some situations, one guideline might indicate that the law of supply and demand will apply while another guideline will say it won't apply. For instance, if Coke drops its price, Pepsi will too. The result will be more overall soft drink sales for both companies because sales for discretionary products do increase with a price decrease. However, the number of sales would not be nearly as high as Coke and Pepsi would expect if only one had dropped its price.

Lower Prices with Caution

There are two reasons to be cautious about lowering prices. First, most products can't maintain the same dollar profit after a price decrease, and second, a reduced price lowers your product's image. If a product sells for $100 and it costs $50 to produce, the profit is $50 and the product has a 50 percent margin. If the price is dropped 10 percent, the profit is only $40. To maintain the profits, a company with a 50 percent margin needs to increase unit sales by 25 percent. That is a difficult sales increase to maintain in a competitive market—and 10 percent is not a large price discount. A 20 percent price discount requires a 66 percent sales volume increase to maintain profits. The arithmetic doesn't work in favor of a price discount. An example of the havoc price discounting can cause is the airline industry. During the years of big airline discounts, virtually every airline lost money.

What about supermarkets and department stores? Both constantly run discount programs. Are they immune to losing profits from price discounting? No. What supermarkets do is promote a few items on sale. When a person gets to the store, most of the products are at full price. The supermarket counts on customers buying full-priced merchandise along with the discounted items. The supermarket's actual discount on most customers' total purchase is actually quite low.

The second reason to be cautious about dropping a price is that the value of a product is determined, to a great extent, by the product's price. Some businesses such as Mercedes Benz, designer jean manufacturers, fancy restaurants, or Bloomingdale's set prices deliberately high to enhance the business's elite image. Other companies have low prices to complement their images, such as K mart, "the saving place." Sears uses mid-range pricing to help position itself as the store for middle-America. Buick and Pontiac are priced about 5 percent above Chevrolet to coordinate with their image as premium cars.

Before you drop a price, always consider what the price discount will do to a product's image. An example of how hard it is to raise a product's image once it is established is the Minnesota Kicks soccer team. The first year the Kicks were in business they charged only $2 or $3 per ticket. Forty thousand people came to every game, and they all had a great time. The next year the Kicks raised the ticket price to the league average of $8 to $10 per ticket. The Kicks didn't last the season. Customers couldn't accept that a ticket to a Kicks game was worth $8 to $10 because they had already set the value of a ticket at $2 to $3.

What Is Your Price Limit?

Every product has a price that can't be exceeded without having sales fall dramatically. You will want to evaluate a product's price history as well as its competitors' history to see how close to its price limit the product is. A product usually has two price limits, one an upper price limit and the other a percentage price premium or discount from competition. For example, a Zenith TV might have an upper price limit of $595. When Zenith is priced over $595, sales fall. Zenith might also need to be priced at least 5 percent below comparable Sony TVs. If Zenith raises its price any closer than 5 percent to Sony's price, its sales will drop.

Another point to consider is products that are slightly different but can still be substituted for a product. For example, Zenith might find that its 25-inch color TVs can't be priced more than 30 percent above 19-inch color TVs.

As an example of establishing a price limit, let's look at a fictitious ski resort, Ski Mountain in the Poconos. The Poconos are a small mountain area about two hours from both New York City and Philadelphia. For readers unfamiliar with ski resorts, prices are usually determined by two features: first, how high the mountain is (vertical lift) that the resort is located on, and second, how many slopes the resort has.

Price/Feature Analysis Of Pocono Ski Resorts

	Vertical Lift	# of Slopes	1988 Price
Ski Mountain	800 feet	18	$22.50
Shady Slopes	800 feet	20	$22.50
Family Paradise	600 feet	12	$16.00
Mount Snowtop	1,000 feet	36	$25.00
Ridge Resort	900 feet	14	$21.00

Skiers in the New York and Philadelphia areas also have the option of going to ski resorts in New England. Those resorts are two to three times larger than the Pocono resorts, but skiers have an additional four- to eight-hour drive to get to them.

FIGURE 3–2

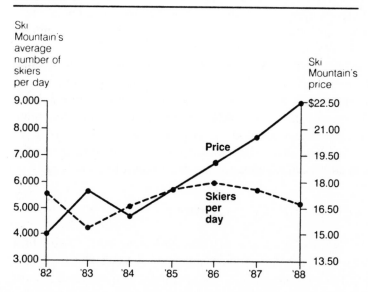

In 1983, Ski Mountain set its price at $17.00, equal to Mount Snowtop's price. Business dropped dramatically. Skiers didn't perceive that Ski Mountain had the value of Mount Snowtop because Ski Mountain had less vertical lift and fewer slopes. Once Ski Mountain set its price 10 percent below Mount Snowtop, sales picked up. The volume drop in 1987 and 1988 was also experienced by all other Pocono resorts except Family Paradise. The decrease in business coincided with most of the Pocono resorts raising their prices to over $20.00. Ski Mountain's two price limits are: first, an upper limit of $20.00, and second, Ski Mountain's price must be 10 percent lower than Mount Snowtop's price.

Incidentally, when you have to retreat from a poor marketing position, try to get as much benefit out of the retreat as possible. I'd recommend that Ski Mountain offer a $5 premium through McDonald's or a large grocery chain.

What Value Are Various Features of Your Product?

Most products have a certain value associated with each product feature. As an example, consider large retail stores. K mart has inexpensive merchandise and a low ambience store layout to go with its low prices. Bloomingdale's, on the other hand, has expensive merchandise, a luxurious store layout, and excellent service to go with its high prices. If you look at retail stores in an area, there will be a series of escalating features along with escalating prices. You should be able to determine a value for each feature. Starting with K mart prices as a base, you might add a 5 percent premium for an improved store layout, a 5 percent premium for sales clerks throughout the store, a 5 percent premium for specialized merchandise, and so on. You also need to remember to include intangible features such as product reliability and name recognition. An additional example of a feature values chart is shown in Figure 3-3.

The purpose for developing a feature values chart is to determine if a product's price/value relationship is perceived by customers to be high or low. Knowing that tells you if a price needs adjustment or if a product needs additional features for the price you'd like to charge.

HOW TO ADD VALUE TO A PRODUCT

The two types of products that are easiest to market are (1) a well-differentiated, premium product and (2) a product that has much higher name recognition than its competitors. Unfortunately, most

FIGURE 3-3

Value of Various Clothes Dryer Features

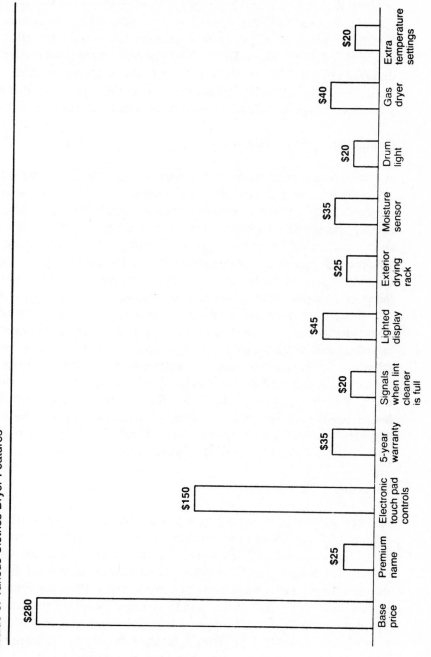

products do not fit into either category. Most products are average, with similar features and name recognition as their competitors. In this situation, a marketer needs to add value to a product. Often marketers try to do this by discounting prices. Discounting prices, as mentioned earlier, has disadvantages and should be used with caution. There are three other tactics you can use to add value without discounting a price: nonmonetary price discounts, targeting a new market, or adding product features.

Nonmonetary Price Discounts

A nonmonetary price discount is a service or feature that you offer a customer without changing the base price of a product. Nonmonetary discounts help improve a product's price/value relationship without tarnishing the product's image. Chrysler offers special option packages, such as automatic transmission, power steering, power brakes, and rear window defogger at a special package price. The package price doesn't change the price of the basic car but adds value for the customer because the price of a package is lower than purchasing each option separately.

Sears catalog policy of taking any product back is a nonmonetary discount that enhances Sears's image. Appliance stores offer nonmonetary discounts when they offer free microwave cooking classes with a microwave purchase. My father's drugstore keeps complete drug records for a nursing home he does business with. This service doesn't change my father's price, but it adds value for the nursing home which no longer needs to keep extensive records. A final example is the hotels that have suites instead of rooms. Those hotels don't charge more than other upscale hotels, but they offer more value to the customer.

Targeting a New Market

Another tactic that works when a product has an average price/value relationship is targeting a new market where the product will have more value. One way to target a new market is to drop a few features and position the product at the top end of a lower-priced market. Dodge did this with its Aries America cars when it dropped two features. First, the 1988 Aries was the same as the 1987 Aries, and Dodge made this clear to customers. The second feature Dodge dropped was an unlimited selection of options; now a person could buy the Aries America with only two or three option packages. As a result of these changes, Dodge could drop the price $1,500, placing the car at the top end of the economy car market.

Another way to target a new market is to add a few features that position the product for another market segment. For example, a hotel by my home converted three of its twelve floors into theme suites. During the week they rented the suites to traveling executives for meetings, and on the weekends the hotel offered special packages for the theme suites, including champagne dinners, shows, and Sunday brunch. The move not only improved the hotel's occupancy rates, but the new suites allowed the hotel to charge a higher price.

Adding Product Features

Adding new features can help improve a product's perceived value as well as help differentiate it. The ideal features to add are ones that are important to the customer and at the same time are inexpensive to add. My favorite way of determining what features to add is to use the ultimate goal model from Chapter 2 (pages 23–24). For every product, determine the two or three goals the customer has when buying a product. For example, when a customer buys a car, the three goals may be ease of use, performance, and aesthetics. Then for each goal, list every feature you can think of that helps the customer reach the goal. As an example, I'll consider the steps needed for a car to be easy to use.

Features Needed for an Easy-to-Use Car

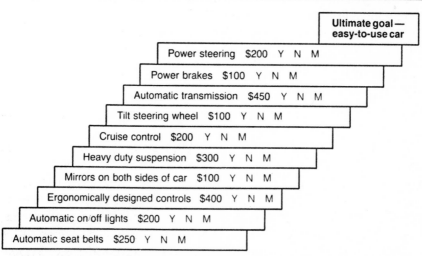

Price listed after each feature is its estimated price. Y = Yes, N = No, M = Maybe. Prospective customer determines if he or she feels a feature is worth the estimated price.

You want to use the ultimate goal chart as a market research tool. Ask customers to:

- Decide if each feature is worth the estimated price.
- Check off the features a car absolutely must have to be easy to use.
- Add any additional features they would like to see.

Once you complete the survey, you will get an idea of what features are worth to customers. Compare customers' perceived value to your costs of providing the feature. Often there will be one or two features that can be economically added to improve a product's value.

I've never done a survey where customers didn't come up with some excellent suggestions of features to add that I hadn't thought of before. This is the real value of the ultimate goal model; it gives the customer a framework for evaluating what features he or she wants. In this example, the customer is thinking of what makes the car easy to use, and you help the customer concentrate even more by listing five to ten easy-to-use features. Customers probably wouldn't have any input if you asked them what features they wanted on a car without the framework of the ultimate goal model.

I've been able to get results with a survey of 50 to 100 prospective customers. On occasion, I've only been able to get surveys from 10 people and have still generated useful information. Market research firms will tell you that a much larger sampling is needed, and no doubt a larger sampling will improve the survey's accuracy. But don't be afraid to run a survey of a few customers if that's all you can get.

CHAPTER 4

PLACEMENT—GETTING YOUR PRODUCT TO CUSTOMERS

UNDERSTANDING PLACEMENT

A product, no matter how great, won't be purchased unless customers can find it. The steps involved in making a product available to its customers are referred to as either *placement* or *distribution* strategies. My experience has been that placement is an often overlooked area of marketing. A common misconception is that a desirable product will sell if it is advertised and promoted. That statement is true, provided the customer can find it; otherwise, no sale will occur.

For example, A&W ran a commercial for a new cream soda. I happen to like cream soda, so I went to two nearby stores looking for A&W's cream soda. Neither store had it, and A&W lost a sale.

Placement is the path between a product and its customers.

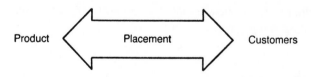

Product   Placement   Customers

Advertising and promotion are tactics that make a product more desirable. More customers seek out a product as it becomes desirable, but the customers still have to be able to find it. Note that on the placement diagram the arrow goes both ways. Sometimes a placement strategy helps a customer come to the product; other times a placement strategy takes the product to the customer.

THE MARKETING MIX

Placement, product, and promotion are the three tactics marketers use to create customer demand. The three tactics are usually referred to as the marketing mix. A brief description of each tactic follows.

Placement. Placing the product into the market in a way that both enhances the product's image and makes the product easy for the customer to buy.

Product. Designing and modifying the product so it offers customers what they want.

Promotion. Advertising, positioning, and other promotions increase the perceived price/value relationship of a product.

A marketer typically has a fixed amount of resources that he or she can use to market a product. Every product has a price limit. A company needs to limit the total dollars spent on marketing a product so the company can profitably price the product and still be below the price limit. The term *mix* is important because a marketer generally cannot increase spending on one element of the marketing mix without reducing the impact of one or both of the other elements.

For example, food at a convenience store such as 7-Eleven is more expensive than food at a supermarket. The price is higher because convenience stores' placement strategy of having several stores in a neighborhood is expensive. Convenience food stores sacrifice a product feature—low supermarket prices—to pay for the placement strategy.

Effective placement strategies are important not only because a marketer must get his product to the market, but also because the level of spending on placement affects how much a company can spend on both the product and its promotion.

WHAT'S IN THIS CHAPTER?

There are dozens of possible placement strategies; in fact, placement covers a wider variety of strategies than any other area of marketing. Yet, often a company's placement strategy is simply a copy of a competitor's strategy. Many companies don't know how to determine the best placement strategy for their product. The goal of this chapter is to help you evaluate both current and potential placement strategies.

The chapter is divided into six sections:

1. Examples of placement strategies: a quick look at five different types of strategies to give you a better feel for what placement strategies are.
2. Evaluating your placement strategy: how to determine if your placement strategy fits your product and its customers. This section covers the principle of placement specialization, a concept important to every business.
3. Location: how retailers can evaluate how well their product fits their location.
4. Professional practices: how professionals can use placement strategies to enhance credibility.
5. Distribution: how manufacturers should assess their distribution channels.
6. Salesforce: how to determine if you're getting the most out of your sales force.

EXAMPLES OF PLACEMENT STRATEGIES

Supermarket Chain

A supermarket has a layout that customers enjoy, but the layout is expensive. The chain has placed its stores in slightly out-of-the-way locations where the rent is lower in order to keep prices competitive with other supermarkets.

Young Pediatrician

A young pediatrician starts her practice in a medical office building in a new suburban tract, but her practice income is not meeting her expectations. Her problem is that there are not enough potential patients in the suburban development. Her placement solution is to open a satellite office in another development four miles away.

Consumer Electronics Company

The company sells low- to mid-priced products through discount appliance and electronics products stores. Two years ago, the company introduced a new state-of-the-art product through the company's standard distribution outlets.

The company had hoped that the new product would elevate the image of the company's entire line of products, but the product never lived up to the company's expectations. The company failed to realize that the distribution channel is just as important to a company's image as a product's features. The new product should have been used to penetrate more prestigious outlets, such as upscale department stores.

Industrial Equipment Supplier

The supplier introduced its product 18 months after similar products were introduced by three competitors. The supplier's market share in other product lines had dropped from 25 to 17 percent without this key product. All the suppliers in this market sold through manufacturer's agents. The supplier didn't feel it could be successful just using agents because it had lost too much market momentum. Instead, the supplier put its own salespeople in key areas to work with two or three agents each. The two-prong strategy offered the customer sales contact continuity with the agent, and offered the customer the superior technical expertise of the industrial equipment supplier's salesforce.

Toy Store

A couple decided to open a unique toy store with expensive toys for children as well as adults after seeing a similar, successful store in another city. The store they were going to imitate was in a slightly out-of-the-way location. The couple determined that the original store had loyal customers from its 30 years in business and therefore didn't need a premium location. Their store, on the other hand, would be unknown and would need a location that encouraged people to come into the store. Thus, the couple decided to open their store in an upscale mall.

HOW TO EVALUATE YOUR PLACEMENT STRATEGY

How do you know if a placement strategy is appropriate? I like to evaluate the effort involved in selling a product and then determine if the placement strategy provides enough effort, or the term I prefer instead of effort, *placement specialization.*

Examples of placement strategies with high and low specialization follow:

In the retail area, gas stations, convenience food stores, and drugstores have low specialization. Car dealerships, expensive clothing, and computer stores have high specialization.

In industrial sales, a product sold through distributors with minimum technical support has low specialization. A product requiring technical presentations by a company's salesforce has high specialization.

In consumer products, a portable radio needs a placement strategy with low specialization, while a high-tech stereo system needs a strategy with high specialization.

In professional practices, a family practitioner who attracts patients from a two-mile radius has low specialization. A dermatologist who attracts patients from a wide area is highly specialized.

What does low or high specialization mean to a placement strategy? If a product requires low specialization, the focus is on getting the product where the customer can easily find it. For example, a newspaper stand just needs a location where a lot of people walk by. The stand doesn't have to be better than a stand three blocks away as long as it is reasonably price competitive. On the other hand, a product that requires a specialized placement strategy requires a lot of effort to sell the product. Customers will also go out of their way to shop at the right store and to buy the right product.

There are two ways to specialize a placement strategy. The first is to have a method of providing support and information for the customer. A stereo store could offer a large inventory, or a capital equipment manufacturer could stress technical backup and service. The second way to specialize a strategy is to take the product to the customer. Life insurance companies take their product to the customer through direct mail and home visits. Candy manufacturers attract customers by placing their product next to a store's checkout line. Candy sales are probably two or three times higher than they would be at another location in the store. Fanny Farmer candy stores have a similar strategy: they are in locations with high foot traffic.

It is essential to have the proper level of specialization in your placement strategy. A specialized strategy may be expensive, and if it's not needed, your cost will be too high. For example, one kiosk in a mall was successful selling inexpensive jewelry to teenagers. Then the operation moved into a store in order to offer more inventory—a more specialized strategy. But the higher rent and larger inventory forced the store to raise its prices, which caused sales to drop dramatically.

On the other hand, sales will be disappointing if a product needs a specialized strategy and doesn't have it. For example, a jewelry store recently opened near my home, but it doesn't have that luxurious look a jewelry store should. The shop is also small with a limited inventory. The store hasn't been successful to date because it doesn't have a specialized approach. Interestingly enough, I've seen another jewelry store that looks just like this one that's doing well. The difference? That store in on Philadelphia's Jewelers' Row. Its location offers a specialized strategy because Jewelers' Row has 15 to 20 jewelry stores on one block.

There are four guidelines you should follow to determine if your level of specialization is appropriate:

Guideline	Low Specialization	High Specialization
How important is the product?	Unimportant	Important
How necessary is the product?	Necessary	Unnecessary
How frequent is the purchase?	Frequent	Infrequent
How technical is the product?	Not very	Very

How Important Is the Product?

Buying a car is an important purchase decision. Before buying, customers will research various models in addition to comparison shopping at several car dealerships. On the other hand, when people buy gas they will usually purchase it at the most convenient station.

The placement strategy for a car manufacturer is to sell through outlets which can provide the support a car buyer wants. A large inventory, trained sales staff, and complete service department are part of the specialization required. The car manufacturer has to worry more about having the proper level of support than it needs to worry about having convenient dealer locations. In contrast, gas companies need to have as many convenient gas stations as the market can support.

Remember too that it is not the product alone that is important, but the solution it provides. Wallpaper is important because it contributes to the way a room looks; my wife spends weeks shopping for wallpaper. Most people don't think a nice looking lawn is as important as a nice looking room; that's why Scott's tries to get its fertilizer into as many outlets as possible.

Sears demonstrates a poor placement strategy when it stocks its indoor paint next to its hardware department. This nonspecialized strategy may have worked years ago when home decorating needs were simpler, but the strategy is all wrong for today's market. Sherwin Williams has a better strategy: it places its paint in home decorating centers with wallpaper and window treatments.

An industrial manufacturer with an easy-to-use, noncrucial product sells its product effectively through distributors and manufacturer's agents. However, if the manufacturer sells a product that is important to customers' productivity, it will typically sell through a dedicated salesforce that can offer customers technical support.

Residential real estate agencies have one of the worst placement strategies I've seen. For most people, a home is the most important investment they'll ever make. However, instead of using a specialized placement strategy with plenty of information for customers, real estate agencies use the nonspecialized strategy of having many small offices.

In 1982, when my wife and I moved to Philadelphia, we weren't sure where we wanted to live, so we went to a real estate office to learn about the market. Listed below are a few of the questions we asked and the answers we received:

What are the values for comparable houses in various neighborhoods?
Oh, the homes are priced a little higher in this neighborhood and a little lower in that neighborhood. If you want to look through the MLS book, we can pick out some homes to look at.
Do you have an up-to-date price study of homes in various neighborhoods?
No.
What is the ranking of the areas' school districts?
The ones in this area are pretty good.

The real estate office just couldn't provide the information my wife and I wanted. We spent over a week gathering information so we could make a somewhat informed decision. Obviously, real estate companies need a more specialized placement strategy.

How Necessary Is the Product?

Do you know where the nearest title insurance company is located? Have you ever had a title insurance company call you? Probably not. But if you buy a house, you must buy title insurance. A title insurance company needs as many real estate agents as possible to recommend it.

The same situation doesn't exist for life insurance. Many people don't think they need life insurance, so life insurance agents bring their product to the customer, usually at his or her home. Bringing a product to the customer's home is a high degree of placement specialization.

Consider the difference between convenience and gourmet food stores. Convenience stores are located almost anywhere there is high traffic, and usually there is just one checkout clerk. The placement strategy doesn't need to be specialized because the customer is buying an item he or she needs. Gourmet food, on the other hand, is not necessary. Some gourmet meat companies use the same tactic as life insurance companies and send agents to customers' homes. Other gourmet shops are located among various specialty shops. The store layout usually has a varied inventory, and the sales clerks typically can provide information about different products.

Professionals (doctors, dentists, and lawyers) tend to forget that they are offering two products. One is a necessity for people who are sick, have a toothache, or are being sued. But professionals also offer preventive care which many customers feel is unnecessary. Placement strategies of most professionals are controlled by their first product.

If a physician wants patients to take preventive physicals, he or she needs to take the product to the customer. Some examples of what a physician could do follow:

> Set aside one or two days a month for physicals only. To make the physicals more enticing for patients, the physician could coordinate his efforts with labs and other needed services to assure his patients that complete physicals would take only an hour.
>
> Work out arrangements with local companies for employee physicals.
>
> Offer a health screening day through a church or community group.

Novels are another example of a specialized strategy. Since novels are not a necessary product, they are sold in prominent displays at grocery stores, airports, and drugstores. The key to a bookseller's success is placing books so they can be spotted by customers for an impulse purchase.

How Frequent Is the Purchase?

Customers need more assurance when a product is purchased infrequently, and therefore a more specialized strategy is required. When people buy a TV, they like to go to a store with a wide variety of TVs on display. It helps to have knowledgeable salespeople as well as in-store information that describes features of the different TVs. When I purchased a lawnmower, I looked first at a nearby home center where there were only two models on display. That just wasn't enough options for me. I didn't feel I would be making a smart buying decision when I had so few models to choose from; so I went to a lawnmower store with 40 models. A wide variety of inventory is one reason that Sears does well with garden equipment—it is one of the few stores that stock a large inventory.

When I buy beer, a frequent purchase, I just go to the most convenient liquor store. I don't care where I buy it as long as the store's prices are reasonable. I don't even care what beer the store carries, as I'll drink any of five or six brands.

How Technical Is the Product?

Customers need to be reassured that they are making a wise purchase decision when buying a technical product that they don't understand. Again, customer reassurance calls for a specialized placement strategy. When food processors were first introduced, they were sold by upscale department stores with well-trained sales personnel. Once food processors were on the market for a while, customers understood the product's positive and negative features, and they were no longer a technical purchase. Consequently, food processors were sold at a wide variety of sales outlets. Food processors might not have succeeded without this two-step strategy.

Examples of Applying the Four Guidelines

1. Grocery Stores

Many shoppers spend one to two hours a week in a grocery store. Grocery costs are also a significant part of most people's monthly budget.

Both factors indicate groceries are an important purchase, therefore requiring a high degree of specialization. On the other hand, grocery purchases are necessary, frequent, and nontechnical. That dictates a placement strategy with low specialization.

Grocery stores need to be conveniently located because of their low specialization features, but they also need to be specialized with a large product selection or an appealing store layout.

2. Fireplace supplies

Recently, at a store that sells fireplace inserts, I saw an iron heat reflector that limited the amount of heat escaping through the chimney.

The product called for a specialized placement strategy because it might be considered a one-time, unnecessary purchase. Thus, the fireplace shop, a specialized outlet, provides an appropriate placement strategy.

LOCATION, LOCATION, LOCATION

Placement and product strategies are closely intertwined for a retail store. A retailer needs a different type of location for each different type of product. Since many retailers choose their product strategy based on their location, I'll look first at having the right product for a location.

I have five wallpaper stores in my immediate area. The first, in a high-traffic mall, offers wallpaper that's both attractive and expensive. The store's displays catch the eye of window shoppers and prompt them to come into the store. I try to keep my wife from walking by so I don't get any new projects. This store gets its customers by appealing to window shoppers.

The second store is in a medium-size building in an offbeat location. It offers an extensive variety of wallpaper patterns at a discount. The store also carries a large inventory of manufacturer's closeouts. Customers go out of their way to get to this store because of its large inventory.

The third store is in an enormous building on a busy street. The store is a wallpaper outlet, but it also carries a wide variety of decorating products and supplies, such as switch covers, lamps, floor tile, chair rail woodwork, paint, and so on. This store depends on its package of decorating services to draw customers.

The fourth store is part of a paint shop on a low-traffic street, but the store constantly offers wallpaper classes, loans out equipment to help customers wallpaper, and gives advice over the phone. The store's level of service is extraordinary, and that service is what helps it keep customers.

The fifth store is another paint shop. It must have had some extra space and then decided to add wallpaper. The store has poor selection, high prices, and poor service. Fortunately, the store has a strong paint business.

The first four stores are examples of smart marketing based on location. In all four cases, the stores developed a product that would draw customers to their locations.

Retailers should decide what type of store they want and then find the right location. The example near the beginning of this chapter about the couple who decided to open a toy store is an example of how to pick the right location. If you are starting a business, try to avoid the common mistake of passing over the right location because the rent is too high. The owner of the new business often feels he or she can move once the business is established. But if a business doesn't have the right location, it needs to offer more of something, and then promote that aggressively to get customers. In the end, the promotion may cost more than renting the right location in the first place, not to mention how easy it is to make a mistake with a promotional program.

PROFESSIONAL PRACTICES

Professionals often associate marketing with advertising. As a rule, professionals don't like advertising because it cheapens their image. But that doesn't mean that professionals shouldn't do marketing; in fact, professionals need to pay particular attention to placement strategies.

Let's go back to the definition of placement—the path between a product and its customers.

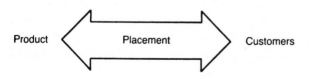

Product   Placement   Customers

Placement strategies should make the path easy for a customer to take and at the same time enhance a product's image.

Professionals need a strategy of placement specialization because customers feel professionals' services are important. The professional's product includes service, knowledge, skill, integrity, and compassion. A professional's placement strategy has to help customers realize the professional has those qualities.

Television's McKensie and Brackman, the firm on "L.A. Law," utilizes both effective and ineffective placement strategies. On the plus side, the office is located in the heart of the city's business district in a building with many prestigious law firms. The lawyers' personal offices look comfortable and attractive. Both of these placement factors inspire customer confidence that the law firm is competent.

However, customers won't be pleased with the chaos they encounter when they walk through the front doors of McKensie and Brackman. This chaos is going to make a client feel that he or she won't get the specialized attention or compassion he or she wants.

Consider three young attorneys who want to start a law firm. None are well known, but their goal is to eventually have a prestigious practice. One attorney wants to open the practice in a small community which is the county seat where rent is lower. The problem with this strategy is that the lawyers won't be establishing a prestigious reputation in a county seat, and they will have trouble changing their image once it is established.

The second attorney wants to obtain space in the most prestigious building in the city. He also suggests hiring a retired bank president to enhance the firm's image of competence and help generate awareness of the firm among potential clients. The strategy has two risks: first, the firm might have trouble being noticed among so many law firms in the building, and second, the strategy places too much emphasis on the retired banker who may leave the firm.

The third attorney wants the firm to specialize in business law. He wants to open the practice in a well-known building that is close to the city's downtown business club. The attorney wants the three of them to join the local business club and volunteer for community projects. This attorney also wants to hire the retired bank president.

The third attorney's plan offers the best placement strategy. First, it works hard to make it easy for clients to find the firm. The practice would be in a well-known building, have the benefit of the retired bank president, and have the attorney's high community profile to help potential clients get to know them. The strategy also enhances the lawyers' image. The building and bank president both add status, while the attorneys' community involvement may give potential clients the impression that the law firm is bigger than it really is.

Professionals should note, too, in their placement strategies that often clients feel comfortable patronizing professionals who they think are like them. Professionals should try to set up their practices where customers' personalities, age, cultural background, and special interests are similar to the professionals'.

Medical Practices

From a marketing point of view, there are two types of medical practices. The first, family physicians and pediatricians, are practices where the customer wants a doctor who is friendly, competent, and nearby. The second type of practice is the specialist, where the patient wants to have the best physician available.

A family physician should be a visible, integral part of a community. However, I think it is a mistake for a physician to open a practice in his home because doing so just doesn't create the competent medical image that a clinic can. I'm also not sure it is wise for a young physician to take over the practice of an older physician. That practice may be in an older neighborhood and depend on older patients. A young physician should open a clinic in an area where he or she can attract younger patients.

A specialist's placement strategy is completely different than a family physician's. A patient might like to have a friendly specialist, but what the patient wants most is an excellent physician; therefore, it is important for the specialist to be associated with an outstanding hospital or medical school.

I think a young specialist should try to become associated with an older specialist. This partnership will help establish the young specialist's credibility in spite of his or her age.

A professional's placement strategy is a critical determinant of his or her success. Professionals can't overcome a poor placement strategy with an aggressive promotion or price strategy the way a retail store can.

YOUR DISTRIBUTION CHANNEL—IS IT WORKING?

Do You Have Control?

An effective placement strategy leaves the manufacturer in control of the sales process, usually through a combination of "push" and "pull" marketing programs and distribution strategy.

A pull marketing program is where a manufacturer tries to create demand so that customers ask for its product. A push program offers incentives to distributors so they sell one manufacturer's product with more vigor than other manufacturers' products.

Consider a compact disc (CD) player manufacturer. CD players are sold to consumers through outlets that carry players from many manufacturers. A manufacturer's first preference is to have enough customer pull so that its product is always requested. If a manufacturer can generate pull demand, it can place its players in premier sales outlets such as department stores, which usually carry only the top three or four brands. Placing a product in premier outlets generates sales at those outlets and also enhances the product's image at secondary outlets.

For example, Serta and Sealy, the two largest mattress manufacturers, have strong customer pull due to both their reputations and advertising programs. Both companies sell through large department, furniture, and bedding stores, but Serta and Sealy also sell through discount bedding stores. Those stores do not like to push Serta and Sealy because they get larger discounts on off-brands. But Serta and Sealy still sell in the discount bedding stores because they have pull, not only from advertising, but from their placement in the better-known stores.

If you have strong pull demand for a product, you must place your product in premier outlets to maximize sales. You must also demand that the secondary outlets display your product prominently. A threat to stop selling to an outlet is powerful when you have strong customer demand for your product. You are in the position of being able to insist you get your desired floor space.

You can't always create strong pull demand. A CD player manufacturer's second preference is to create a "pull-push" demand program. A pull-push program requires that customers are familiar with a product, creating pull, while at the same time offering enough promotional discounts to the distributor to create push demand. Whirlpool washing machines are an example of a pull-push program. Whirlpool advertises enough so people know who it is and that it makes a good product. Then Whirlpool offers incentives to a sales outlet to become an authorized Whirlpool dealer. Whirlpool products are featured throughout the outlet, and usually the outlet will feature Whirlpool in its promotional literature.

When you have enough customer demand to create a pull-push program, aim for the second tier of distribution outlets, which for a CD player manufacturer are catalog showrooms, discount consumer electronics outlets, and small music stores. Work on setting these outlets up as authorized distributors. Be sure you get a certain percentage of the distributor's business and that the outlet will feature your product in a prominent display. You should also try to set a limit on how many different brands of your product the outlet will carry.

Sometimes a manufacturer doesn't have enough customer demand to create either a pull or a pull-push placement program. Then a manufacturer must try to get in as many distribution outlets as possible. Usually a manufacturer without customer demand must give large discounts as well as control of its business to the distributor. A manufacturer in this situation should start working immediately on creating customer demand. If you don't have customer demand, it may take one or two years to create it. Don't drop your push marketing programs too quickly.

Do You Have the Right Number of Outlets?

Sometimes your sales are limited by not having enough distribution outlets. For instance, if you sell beer and only 5 percent of the bars in an area have your beer on tap, your sales may be limited. Sales may increase more by adding outlets than by increasing consumer demand.

The possibility of sales being limited by the number of outlets does not mean that the more outlets a product has, the better off it is. What counts is the quality of the sales and how those outlets support a marketing strategy. In order to constantly monitor and support outlets so they offer support of a marketing program, you must have your salesforce spend enough time with each outlet. I don't think it hurts to have a salesperson call on an outlet once a week. You and the outlet are partners; you need to work together. It's important that you have only as many outlets as you can work with closely.

For example, at the dental company I worked for, one salesperson met every week for breakfast with a key distributor. They talked about problems, opportunities, and how they could work together to increase sales. The breakfasts helped the distributor because the salesperson always came up with new ideas for the distributor. The breakfasts helped the salesperson because the distributor was increasing sales of his product. The breakfasts benefited the company because the salesperson pushed programs that enhanced the company's image. The close working relationship eventually made this distributor the top-selling distributor of our products in the country.

Do Distributors Support Your Product?

Distributors can be placed into three broad categories:

1. Those who support your product.
2. Those who sell your product.
3. Those who promote someone else's product.

No matter how much customer pull demand a company creates, it is going to have distributors that do not perform well. Periodically evaluate your distributors, and put them into one of the three categories. Carefully monitor distributors to make sure your product is receiving quality support. If a product is losing category 1 distributors, the lost volume can't be made up by adding distributors in categories 2 and 3 without losing some control of the sales process.

One example of a company losing control of the sales process is Firestone. Ten years ago in the Philadelphia area, Firestone had some of its own tire outlets, while other tire dealers featured Firestone tires. Then some large tire discounters opened in Philadelphia, causing Firestone to close its stores. Eventually Firestone lost its featured position at other tire dealers around the city when those dealers were forced to carry off-brands to compete with the discounters.

The first step in generating more support from distributors is to treat them as partners, not as adversaries. The distributor's main interest is selling more than its competitor up the street. Any program you run that helps a distributor make a sale will be mutually beneficial.

I ran a program once that gave distributor salespeople a sales plan along with support materials. The salespeople were able, with these materials, to give a convincing sales presentation on our product. The program worked like a charm; salespeople didn't want to lose customers, and they didn't lose many if they followed the sales plan. The program really wasn't extensive, but the point is that salespeople can't know how to sell every product. I made it easier for them to specialize in selling one.

Other programs that you can use to keep distributors in or move them into category 1 include creative in-store displays, superior service, and co-op advertising.

Let's go back to the Firestone example. What could the company have done to prevent losing its category 1 distributors? First, Firestone should have created in-store displays that showed customers why a Firestone tire was a good buy—something customers could touch and see to understand the difference between a Firestone tire and its cheaper competitors. Second, Firestone should have provided a sales training kit for its dealers' salespeople. And finally, Firestone should have kept improving its product every year to insure that the tires were always a step ahead of the off-brands.

ARE YOU GETTING THE MOST OUT OF YOUR SALESFORCE?

Typically, the value of a salesforce is downplayed by marketers. After all, marketers design brilliant strategies and fantastic promotions to make the salesforce's job easy. But no matter how great a product or marketing campaign is, there is always buyer reluctance. And who gets the customer to buy?—the salesforce.

Now, I imagine some of you are saying that salespeople are important for large-ticket items such as cars or industrial equipment, but not for low-cost consumer items like potato chips or soft drinks. Yet, it's the soft drink company's salesforce that gets the all-important shelf space at the supermarket. The salesforce must overcome supermarket buyers' reluctance to give away prime shelf space.

Two keys to optimizing the use of salespeople are, first, effectively focusing their efforts on key buying influences, and second, giving salespeople the tools they need to sell customers.

How Many Salespeople Do You Have?

You need to coordinate marketing programs with the number of salespeople your company employs. If a competitor has 30 salespeople versus your 10, you just can't offer the same level of support as the other company. And in many cases, sales will be lower due to this lack of support. The effectiveness of your marketing program may also be lessened.

For example, I worked for an industrial chemical company with a salesforce a third the size of its two major competitors. The company's sales were sluggish despite the fact that the salesforce was calling on all major accounts once a month and all other accounts at least once a quarter. To get sales moving, management asked each salesperson to write out an action plan to generate business from key targeted accounts. It turned out that none of the salespeople had enough time to get business from all his or her key accounts. Therefore, the company dropped two of the four markets it had been pursuing and concentrated the efforts of both its marketing programs and salesforce. After a few years, sales grew to the point where the company could add salespeople and attack another target market.

Can Your Salesforce Hit Your Sales Objectives?

Some of my most effective marketing programs have come from this question. At the dental company I worked for, the company wanted to increase sales 15 percent. For the most part, the salespeople worked hard, and sales management didn't feel it was realistic to ask them to increase sales 15 percent. At the same time, most of the salesforce would have protested vehemently if we had cut their territories. So our marketing program centered around giving the salesforce better leads so they could be more productive.

First, every ad we ran requested the dentist to send in for more information. Then we set up a lead fulfillment program where we sent out literature to each respondent and then used telemarketing to contact that respondent every three months. The minute the customer was ready to buy, we sent out a hot lead sheet to the appropriate salesperson. Our salesforce was able to close sales on 50 percent of those leads versus the normal 25 percent.

The lead fulfillment program did something else for our salesforce that we hadn't expected. Until we started the program, our dealers were the only ones who knew which dentists were ready to buy, and they parceled out that information to various suppliers at their discretion. But with the new program, the salesforce often knew about some prospects before the dealer. That knowledge gave the salesforce tremendous leverage and significantly helped sales.

I worked for an industrial test equipment supplier that had a limited number of prospects spread throughout the country. Although the company couldn't afford to make more than one sales call on each prospect, a product like ours typically required from two to four sales calls to get an order. Not surprisingly, the company's sales closing rate was a low 10 percent, which was not high enough to hit the company's sales objectives.

We needed to raise the sales closing rate without increasing the number of sales calls, and we were, in fact, successful in developing a marketing program that eliminated the need for the first two or three sales calls. When a prospect expressed an interest in our product, we would ask for a customer sample and then we modified a detailed 20- to 25-page report so it fit the prospect's application. The report was impressive enough that it would be passed around to all interested people at the prospect's company. When everyone with an influence on the buying decision expressed interest in our product, the salesperson would make the call. This narrowed the prospects we needed to call on and raised our closing rate to over 50 percent.

Marketing programs that help make a salesforce more effective are often inexpensive. The program at the dental company cost $24,000 a year for 2,500 leads. The program at the industrial test equipment company cost less than $2,000. More importantly, sometimes a salesforce can't hit the company's sales objectives. When that happens, try to create a marketing program to help it.

What Sales Tools Are Needed?

I am a staunch believer in having salespeople well equipped with sales tools that help make sales points. As an example of what types of sales tools you might need, I'll take the sales points listed in an ad (*Time*, Aug. 29, 1988, pages 40–41) for a Mazda 929 and list what sales tools are needed.

1. *Sales Point—Exceptional Room and Comfort.* Sales tool needed: Mazda should prepare a chart showing leg and head room for both the front and back seats of the Mazda 929 and its two competitors, the Mercedes-Benz 300E and the BMW 528e.

2. *Sales Point—Fuel Injected V6 Engine.* Sales tool needed: A chart comparing elapsed times for reaching 60 miles per hour for

a V4 engine, a nonfuel-injected V6 engine, and a fuel-injected V6 engine.

3. *Sales Point—Uncommonly Well Equipped.* Sales tool needed: A chart comparing the standard equipment on a Mazda 929 and its two major competitors.

4. *Sales Point—E-link Suspension.* Sales tool needed: A diagram comparing E-link suspension to a competitive suspension system, or better yet, a working model of the E-link suspension system.

5. *Sales Point—Serious Instrumentation.* Sales tool needed: A photo of the instrumentation in the car without a steering wheel blocking the view. Instrumentation that most cars don't have should be highlighted.

Salespeople probably won't use all the sales tools with every prospect, but there will be times when the sales tools will make the difference in closing a sale.

Two other ways of finding out what types of sales tools you need are to make a few of your own sales calls, and to listen to the problems new salespeople are having.

I believe marketing people should make at least a few sales calls every six months. Watch what points the customer accepts and which ones he or she seems skeptical of. Also, try using the sales tools you do prepare to see how customers accept them.

New salespeople's problems also will help you discover needs for sales tools. New salespeople are a better source of information than experienced salespeople because newcomers haven't learned yet how to overcome common customer objections. Sometimes a sales tool will more convincingly overcome a customer objection than anything a salesperson can say.

SUMMARY

I believe placement is second only to the product in importance when preparing an effective marketing strategy; unfortunately, it is often the last consideration in the marketing plan. Discipline yourself to evaluate changes in your placement strategies every time you do a marketing plan.

CHAPTER 5

SURVIVAL ISSUES:
STAYING IN BUSINESS

Three discount grocery stores recently closed in my neighborhood. All three stores had prices 15 to 20 percent below area supermarkets; all three stores seemed busy. Then why did the stores fail? Their prices were too low to generate profits.

In the late 1970s and early 1980s, two or three entrepreneurs entered the greeting card market with funny, all-occasion cards. The entrepreneurs fared well until Hallmark introduced its own line of off-beat cards, causing all the entrepreneurs to lose sales volumes and forcing one out of business. The entrepreneurs' error was that they hadn't developed a defensible strategy that would protect their market position.

General Motors recently announced it was closing several plants. GM's aim was to scale back production to increase profits. In the process, GM's market share is dropping sharply.

Contrast GM's situation to Sewell Cadillac in Dallas, Texas (*Inc.*, May 1988, pages 80–82). Sewell sells 2,500 Cadillacs per year without rebates or incentives. The difference?—momentum. Sewell has it and GM doesn't.

Adequate profits, defensibility, and momentum are the key issues for survival. This chapter covers these topics in five sections:

1. Pricing and sales volume—What does it take to survive?
2. Defensibility—How to protect your market position.
3. Momentum, momentum, momentum—How to keep on top in the market.
4. General Motors—Why America's biggest company is going downhill.
5. Seven-Up—Why its market position is indefensible and what it should have done.

PRICING AND SALES VOLUME—WHAT DOES IT TAKE TO SURVIVE?

Every company needs to cover its expenses and protect its market share position. If a company doesn't cover its expenses, it usually goes out of business. If a company doesn't protect its market share position, it usually has to reduce its size. Marketers are responsible for ensuring both that products can be priced high enough to cover expenses and that company sales volumes will maintain market share. In order to meet those responsibilities, a marketer must know the minimum price and sales volume a company needs to survive.

Some marketers believe that lowering a price below its minimum is acceptable as long as sales volumes increase. I don't agree. As I pointed out in Chapter 3, lowering prices does not guarantee a sales volume increase. If you lower prices and sales volumes don't rise, your company could be out of business. Be cautious and base your minimum price on historical sales levels.

Pricing

Your minimum price must cover both your variable expenses, such as the costs of buying raw materials, and your fixed expenses, such as rent, administrative salaries, and utilities. Some companies have a standard guideline, for example a product's price must be twice the cost of buying or manufacturing it, in order to cover fixed expenses. I prefer to calculate a minimum price with the following formulas:

First calculate the net profit per unit you need to cover fixed and administrative costs:

Net Profit per Unit = (Fixed + Admin. Costs) ÷ Unit Sales

Then use the minimum price formula:

Minimum Price = Net Profit per Unit + Cost of Buying or Manufacturing per Unit + Cost of Marketing and Sales per Unit

Chapter 3 (pages 44–46) covered the perils of dropping a price, emphasizing that it should be done only with great caution. If you are forced by a competitive pressure to drop a price below its minimum, immediately start to discover ways to add value to the product so you can raise its price back above the minimum.

Sales Volume

The sales level needed to hold market share and the sales level needed to maintain profitability are the two criteria for determining the level of sales you need. How your required sales level compares to your actual sales level determines how aggressive your marketing programs should be. If your sales volume is lower than required, you need an aggressive marketing program to increase sales. If your sales volume is adequate, you may want to take a more conservative approach to protect sales.

For example, in the 1970s, American car manufacturers began losing market share to Japanese companies. While they should have been running aggressive programs to block the competitive threat, American car manufacturers' efforts were instead conservative, and sales dropped further to the point where Chrysler needed government loans to survive. On the other hand, Campbell's Soup has a solid market share position even though its marketing programs are cautious. Campbell's introduces a few new soup variations every year or two and just keeps emphasizing that "Soups are good food."

Three other factors that influence the required sales volume also can help you determine how aggressive a marketing program should be. They are:

1. Importance of the product.
2. Rate of growth in the market.
3. Competitive pressures.

If a product is important to your company's sales, you need to protect its sales volumes. As long as a product is not losing market share, its marketing programs should focus on improving the product's defensive position in the market. If a product provides only a small percentage of a company's sales, it can take a more daring strategy; if the strategy doesn't work, it doesn't hurt the corporation, while if it does succeed, it can help substantially. An example is Walt Disney's Touchstone Films. The company was originally a small part of the Disney empire, and Disney could afford to take a risk and produce nonfamily-oriented movies. Touchstone was successful and is now an important asset to Disney.

If a market is growing rapidly, you can take a more aggressive marketing approach because competitors are not as likely to counter your moves. On the other hand, if a market is mature, competitors will typically respond to your every move, which might cause a program to fail. For example, when video rental stores first opened, the market expanded rapidly. In Philadelphia, West Coast Video opened a chain of stores and became the dominant video rental store advertiser. The small independents didn't respond because their sales also were increasing. When the market matured, West Coast Video had the market strength to start pushing the independents out of the market. If West Coast Video had waited until the market matured, the independents would have responded to its moves.

Sometimes your sales volume or market share position is threatened by competitive pressures. You should respond aggressively to a competitive threat before it hurts your company's long-term position. Consider Xerox. At one time Xerox was virtually unopposed in the copier market. Then a few companies introduced smaller copiers, and Xerox didn't respond. Now those companies, such as Canon, have a firm foothold in the market and are expanding into the larger-copier market. I even hear people say photocopy now instead of Xerox copy. Xerox should have responded aggressively when the new copiers were introduced.

DEFENSIBILITY—HOW TO PROTECT YOUR MARKET POSITION

How much trouble would a competitor have luring away your customers? If it would be difficult, you have a defensible market position. A defensible position can be the result of a wide variety of factors. Mercedes-Benz has a defensible position because of its name recognition. A card shop might have a defensible position because it's next to the area's most popular supermarket. IBM has a defensible position in mainframe computers because it has the industry's biggest and best salesforce. Walmart discount department stores have a defensible strategy because they are located in markets that are big enough for only one discount store.

The key to a defensible strategy is having a feature or features that a competitor can't duplicate. Consider the offbeat card entrepreneurs I mentioned at the beginning of the chapter. Their position wasn't defensible because Hallmark could introduce a similar line of cards. The entrepreneurs could have created a defensible position by establishing in the people's mind certain characters, such as Ziggy or Cathy, as the focal point of their offbeat cards. Or they might have signed contracts with retail outlets, offering larger discounts in return for a three-year contract.

People's Express is another example of a market position that was not defensible. People's Express built up early sales momentum due to its low prices. But competitors quickly imitated the low prices, driving People's Express out of business.

Product, promotion, placement, positioning, and service are the five areas where most defensible tactics are created. The rest of this section explains how you can develop defensible tactics in each of the five areas. As you read, strive to create a defensible tactic for your business in as many of the five areas as possible.

Product

Product tactics often provide a small company the best defense against a larger competitor. Many product strategies rely on quick turnaround and innovation rather than a significant financial clout.

For example, a Sir Speedy printer by my home constantly adds new services and always attempts to subcontract out any service it doesn't offer. That flexibility is quite a contrast to the large printers in my area, which will only do certain types of printing jobs.

The four defensible product tactics I'll cover are: quality, piggybacking, in-depth product line, and unique product line.

1. Quality

The market's perception of quality has more to do with a product's success than any other factor. Nothing is as effective as quality for keeping customers, and nothing will stop people from buying your product like poor quality. Japanese cars, for example, reap the benefits of high quality. The Renault Alliance, on the other hand, suffers the image of poor quality. (Alliance sales dropped dramatically once it became known that the car had transmission problems.) If your product has high quality, be sure to mention it in your ads and promotional materials.

One of the best ways to improve your perceived quality is to send out questionnaires to customers after they have purchased a product.

I sent out a questionnaire to purchasers of a dental chair and received a 25 percent response. Ninety-five percent of the customers surveyed were happy with the dental chair's quality, but 30 percent listed one particular quality problem. By reacting to that input, we improved the chair's quality image.

2. Piggybacking
Piggybacking is a tactic that associates one product with another product that has a stronger market position. Piggybacking can apply in many ways:

> You sell one product along with a stronger product. Examples are Allstate Insurance's association with Sears, and sales of Levi denim jackets along with blue jeans.

> You have a product with strong distribution channel support that can pull along lesser-known products. An example is the way Coke sells Sprite in vending machines and packages Sprite for fast-food restaurants.

> You can piggyback off a well-known person or place. A law firm might hire a high-profile politician; doctors might teach a course at a university medical school.

> You can piggyback off a stronger company. Retail stores in many small shopping centers piggyback off a supermarket.

> You can piggyback off companies that might be strong in markets where you are weak. For example, a small regional airline, such as Piedmont, sometimes shares frequent flyer coupons with a non-competing airline, such as Northwest, that is strong in another part of the country.

> You can couple your efforts with a company that sells a complementary product. An example is when an airline reservation service offers low rental car rates from one rental car company.

3. In-depth Product Line
Titan Tool is a small manufacturer that sells inspection gauges and microscopes to machine shops. It has an 85-page catalog of every conceivable inspection device and accessory a machine shop could need. Every item adds to Titan Tool's defensible strategy. The in-depth product line is not only difficult for a competitor to copy, but it also enhances Titan's image as the company for every measuring tool need.

Some readers might call Titan's line broad. I don't like to use the term *broad* because it implies a wide variety of products. Titan's success is due to its concentration on one industry.

A law firm would have a broad product line if it included a wide variety of specialists, such as divorce, criminal, and tax lawyers. A law firm's product line is in-depth if it meets all the needs of a certain clientele.

4. Unique Product Line
Some companies have product lines that cannot be easily copied. Polaroid instant cameras have patent protection, thereby eliminating any possible competitors. The Banana Republic retail stores with African safari clothes do well because of their unusual merchandise. Some physicians specialize in one unusual procedure to create a defensible market position.

Promotion

Promotion is often viewed as a short-term activity to generate immediate sales, but a well-designed, consistent promotion program can create a defensible strategy. Examples of promotion tactics that lead to a defensible market position follow:

1. Pizza Pasta
Pizza Pasta is a small pizzeria by my home. It's a little hard to get to, but I always buy pizza there. Why? Every week it has a coupon in our neighborhood newspaper. I can count on Pizza Pasta's consistency.

2. Human Resource Services, Inc.
Human Resource Services is a small personnel consulting firm that has a contract with the Manufacturer's Association of the Delaware Valley (Philadelphia area) to conduct seminars. Every mailing the association makes promotes seminars, keeping Human Resource Services' name constantly before personnel managers in the Philadelphia area.

3. Miller Lite Beer
Miller Lite commercials accomplish three defensible tactics.

> The commercials are consistent. Pro athletes are always shouting "Less Filling" or "Tastes Great." Consistency drives home the message.
>
> Miller runs Lite commercials all the time. Spending heavily on a product adds to its defensibility.

Miller's campaign addresses an important point—that Lite beer tastes great.

These examples demonstrate the three promotion tactics—promote with consistency, promote often, and promote an important point—that make a market position more defensible by making a product memorable. A competitor will have trouble stealing your customers if they remember something positive about your product.

Positioning

I opened my telephone book to look for a furniture store. The stores' ads provide insight into using positioning as a tactic to develop a defensible market position. What I found in the phone book was:

- Thirteen stores that advertised famous-name brands, quality service, and discount prices.
- Six stores that advertised unpainted furniture at discount prices.
- Four stores that advertised contemporary Scandinavian furniture.
- One store that advertised Williamsburg adaptations and reproductions.
- One store that advertised a free interior design service, including the selection of drapes, carpets, window dressings, and slipcovers.

The first two groups of stores promoted discount prices. That's an indication that the stores don't have a defensible positioning strategy. None of the stores in the last three groups advertised discount prices; plus, the stores in those categories appeared distinctly different than the other stores. Full retail prices and strong product differentiation are indications a store has a defensible position.

Differentiating a product adds to its defensibility, but doesn't guarantee it. A more defensible strategy is to position a product as a market leader. Two of the differentiated furniture stores are in the expensive furniture market where they are the leaders. I don't want to downplay the importance of product differentiation because it is an excellent marketing tactic. But if a product isn't one of the top three in a market, it won't have the financial resources to withstand an all-out competitive promotional attack. The sales losses of both RC Cola and 7UP can be at least partially attributed to the promotional war between Coke and Pepsi.

The key to using positioning as a defensive tactic is finding a market where your product can be a leader.

Positioning and niche marketing strategies have been written about for years in business magazines and books—so why do 19 out of 25 furniture stores have a poor positioning strategy? The problem is market size. Many target markets, such as expensive furniture, might be too small to support a company's sales objectives, so the company decides to attack broad markets. It is hard work to find a target market that can both support your sales objectives and allow you to be the market leader, but once you find that market, you will probably be successful. Some well-known examples of profitable products that have found the right market are Jeeps, Chrysler's minivans, Mercedes-Benz autos, Polaroid instant cameras, Walmart discount department stores, Campbell's Soup, and Heinz Ketchup.

Placement

Two young pharmacists bought a Rexall drugstore in Minneapolis. Three years later, a Walgreen's drugstore put them out of business. Most of the Rexall store's customers came from two large apartment towers for senior citizens located seven blocks away. Walgreen's opened its store next to the towers. The young pharmacists didn't have a defensible placement strategy.

The best defensible tactics are often involved with placement. Placement tactics protect a company for a longer period of time than any other tactic. Woolworth's is an example. Fifteen to twenty years ago, 5-and-10-stores started the declining phase in their product life cycle. Only one 5-and-10-store survived—Woolworth's—and it survived simply because it had more stores than its competitors.

Placement tactics to create a defensible market position revolve around three questions: Where is it? What type is it? and How many are there?

1. Where Is It?

About a year ago, I visited a mall with two stores selling fancy soaps and other women's products for the bathroom. One shop, a Crabtree and Evelyn, was on the first floor, two stores away from the mall's main entrance. The other store was on the third floor. Since both stores depended on people walking past, the store with the most passersby was more defensible. If you look at gas stations in your area, you'll find the same situation: the more traffic that passes a gas station, the more likely it is to survive.

A young pedodontist (a dentist for young children) set up his office next to the area's largest pediatrician. This defensible strategy put the pedodontist where he would be easily noticed by a large number of patients.

Another such strategy comes from a life insurance company that has its annuities sold by Merrill Lynch brokerage houses. Again, the place the product is sold exposes it to a large number of potential customers.

2. What Type Is It?

A manufacturer of metallurgical equipment has over a 50 percent market share; a competitor with a similar product has a 15 percent share. The first company sells through its own highly specialized salesforce. The second company sells through manufacturer's agents. The first company's position is more defensible because it has the right type of salesforce for its technical product.

Each of two malls near my home has a fancy gift store. One store appears to be doing well, while the other seems to be struggling. The difference is that the successful store is in an upscale mall where all the stores sell expensive merchandise. The other store is in a mall where stores sell moderately priced merchandise. The right type of location gives the first store a defensible strategy.

3. How Many Are There?

My kids often ask to go to McDonald's, but never to Wendy's. Part, if not all, of the reason for this is that McDonald's has more restaurants than Wendy's. Every time we go by a McDonald's, the kids want to stop. We rarely go by a Wendy's.

GM's sales are three to four times as large as Chrysler's. Does this mean that GM's customers are more loyal than Chrysler's? Or that GM's cars are much better than Chrysler's? No, GM's sales are higher because GM has a bigger dealer network; the large network contributes to a defensible position.

Service

Customers want and appreciate good service. My wife and I always go to an appliance store that's out of our way because it is the only store we've found where the salespeople can explain the differences between various products. My wife and I are not unique; every person I know has at least one store he or she goes to simply because of service.

Overall, the service level in the United States is appalling. That's why service is always an area to look at when searching for a tactic to improve a product's defensibility. I know someone who went to buy a desktop publishing system. He looked at several stores but didn't make a purchase because he couldn't find a salesperson who could prepare a half-page sample. He wasn't sure if the salespeople were untrained or if desktop publishing systems were hard to use, so he was afraid to buy one. A computer store with a trained salesforce would have a defensible strategy.

This example is not unusual. Most people can think of two or three examples of bad service they've had in the last 30 days.

Service is probably the best strategy for keeping current customers. Chapter 9 talks more about service and how you can put it to work for your business.

MOMENTUM, MOMENTUM, MOMENTUM

Most marketing principles have a sound rationale for their importance. The one major exception is momentum. Momentum in the marketplace is much more important than I can explain in a few sentences. A marketer needs to be worried about momentum because it is difficult to regain once it has been lost.

Sony recently stopped selling its Betamax VCR unit. The Betamax was a high-quality, well-differentiated product from a reputable, well-known company. It had, by most standards, an acceptable marketing program. The Betamax had the additional benefit of scoring highly in technical reports. But last year, Sony withdrew the Betamax while 13 million VCRs were being sold.

Betamax was the victim of lost momentum. People buy products that are winners. This goes back to the Chapter 2 discussion on the axiom, "Fear of loss is a greater motivator than opportunity for gain." Once it became clear that sales of the competing VHS technology would exceed Betamax's sales, people started to switch to VHS systems.

One key to momentum is to always look like a winner in the consumer's eye. After all, if you are successful, people will buy from you. The success—implied or real—gives your customers confidence in you.

Looking like a winner can also help you overcome adversity. Consider Tylenol. When cyanide poisoning was discovered in some Tylenol capsules, the company took a positive "can do" approach. The company recalled every bottle, gave full refunds, and developed a new product package. This projected a winning attitude to consumers, and Tylenol is still the market leader.

E. F. Hutton is an example of what happens when a company projects a losing image. First, Hutton's president resigned to go to another brokerage house. Some transaction irregularities then further tarnished Hutton's image. Before 18 months passed, Hutton's sales had fallen sharply, and it was acquired by Shearson Lehman.

Momentum means looking like a winner. This section is broken down into four topics that will help your company look like a winner:

1. Keep your lead product strong.
2. Where will the business come from?
3. Keep your placement strategies strong.
4. Will you be in business forever?

Remember as you read the section that you must always worry about losing momentum. If you wait till it's lost before taking action, it's doubtful you'll recover quickly, if at all. As an example, consider Renault, which had started to build up momentum with its LeCar and later its Alliance. But once Renault ran into quality problems, it lost momentum, and Renault's U.S. operations were sold to Chrysler. Or consider Volkswagen who lost momentum in the early 1980s to Japanese cars. Despite some excellent new models, Volkswagen has never been able to recapture its market share.

Keep Your Lead Product Strong

The dental company I worked for had a 20 percent market share in high-speed drills, and the drills accounted for 40 percent of the company's sales. One year, the company decided it could increase profits by concentrating its new product development on secondary products lines. Within a year, sales of all our products were dropping—a competitor had introduced a new feature in its high-speed drills that our company couldn't match. Customers lost faith in our entire product line because we couldn't keep our lead product strong. Our new products didn't have a chance. We reversed the situation only after introducing a new high-speed drill ourselves.

Ford used a lead product strategy to create market momentum in the early 1980s when it was in trouble. At the time, Ford didn't have a strong product, was being hurt by Pinto lawsuits, and was being chastised by the media for losing money. Then Ford introduced the Escort, promoting it as a world-class car. Actually, the Escort was a basic economy car. Ford may have promoted it heavily out of desperation, but the lead product strategy gave Ford momentum. About three to four years ago, Ford started to promote its Tempos and Thunderbirds as aerodynamic cars. Finally, Ford's efforts paid off with the introduction of the Taurus. Again, a strong lead product helped the entire product line. The Taurus has people believing that Ford knows what it's doing.

The principle of a strong lead product is just as important for a retailer or professional. Sears uses its well-established appliance and hardware departments as its lead products. Law firms use a well-known lawyer or a law specialty as a lead product. A record store might feature compact discs or 50s music as a lead product. Successful restaurants often have a house specialty that serves as a lead product.

A lead product doesn't have to be the product with the highest demand; it just needs to be important or interesting. I saw a store in a mall with an eyecatching window display of miniature perfume bottles. The store also devoted 20 percent of its floorspace to miniatures. The manager told me that 5 percent of his sales were miniatures; the store's big seller was colognes. But the miniatures made the store noticeable and memorable. More importantly, the miniatures gave customers the impression that the store manager understood perfumes.

Many businesses don't have a lead product. They should consider choosing or developing one. It will help define a company's identity and create market momentum.

Where Will Business Come From?

To keep up momentum, a marketer needs to keep every market program working effectively. When a marketing program fails, it detracts from the company's winning image. Sometimes customers don't notice programs that fail, but not having a winning program in front of your customers will also hurt your image.

I've always found that the best way to be sure a program will work and make the company a winner is to ask the question, "Where will the business come from?" If I can answer that question and see that I'll look like a winner, I know I've got an effective program. In fact, the question has saved me from running some poor programs. I'll examine how the question could help form the marketing programs for the Mitsubishi Starion and a CPA.

1. Mitsubishi Starion

Mitsubishi's Starion is a sporty car that is equivalent to Mazda's RX7 or Nissan's 300SX. Mitsubishi introduced the Starion so its product line would resemble Mazda's and Nissan's in an effort to establish Mitsubishi as a viable car company. To date, few Starions have been sold; Mitsubishi's big-selling product is its family sedan, the Galant.

Mitsubishi's marketing department wants every dealer to sell 50 Starions this year. Mitsubishi is going to give each dealer an extra 5 percent discount on Starions as well as provide dealers with a showroom display. Mitsubishi will also run a magazine advertising program. Mitsubishi feels this program gives the dealers enough support to sell 50 cars each. After all, 50 cars for each dealer is a very small percentage of what Mazda and Nissan are selling.

Where will the business come from? Just who will buy the Starion with the proposed campaign? Someone who has read a magazine ad or two? Not likely, since the Starion is not well known. Someone who visits a Mitsubishi showroom and likes the looks of the Starion? Not likely, since 90 percent of the people who visit the showroom are interested in the family sedan Galant. Someone who wants to save 5 percent when buying a Starion instead of an RX7 or 300SX? Not likely, since the RX7 and 300SX have established sports car images while the Starion has yet to develop one.

The potential Mitsubishi program isn't strong enough to convince customers to buy a Starion. It is making the mistake of thinking that any company can get a little market share just by being on the market.

Mitsubishi should decide to introduce the Starion in one market where it can promote the car effectively. It should heavily advertise it, making it clear why the Starion is a better choice than the RX7 and 300SX. Once the Starion succeeds in the first market, it will start to look like a winner.

Whenever introducing a new product, try to go first to a market where you can succeed. Then build off of success. A program that tries to cover too broad a market, such as the proposed Starion plan, is destined to fail.

2. Certified Public Accountant

A certified public accountant (CPA) has been in business two years without meeting his income expectations. He has been unable to attract large companies, who prefer a big name accounting firm. His clients instead are very small companies.

The CPA has identified his target companies as mid-size firms with 10 to 30 employees. To attract their attention, the CPA wants to create a unique service. His first choice was a payroll service, but before starting to market it, the CPA decided to find out where the service's business would come from. He called the president or personnel manager of seven prospective customers to gauge their interest.

The CPA learned that a payroll service wasn't unique. Instead he found that companies were interested in receiving help in obtaining financing. Further surveys indicated 30 percent of his targeted firms were interested in this service. The CPA calculated that he would hit his income objectives if 15 percent of the companies needing financing used his services. That was a realistic goal, and the CPA decided to specialize in helping mid-size companies obtain financing. The CPA's unique service made him look like a winner.

The CPA did something that is always helpful—he checked his program with customers before he implemented it. This has several advantages:

It helps determine if a program will work.

It tells you where the increased business will come from.

Customers often make suggestions that improve the program.

If at all possible, always ask customers what they think of a new marketing program.

Keep Your Placement Strategies Strong

If I were marketing a product and could only have one strong marketing element, in most cases I'd choose placement. Once a strong placement strategy is lost, it can take a long time to get it back.

Less than 10 years ago, U-Haul was the only company renting out moving equipment to people moving themselves. One of U-Haul's strengths was its vast distribution network. Every town had two or three gas stations that rented U-Haul equipment. As traditional gas stations started to be replaced by convenience food stores selling gas or large stations that only sold gas, U-Haul lost some of its placement locations. Though a customer could still rent a U-Haul trailer, he or she had a little more trouble finding one. U-Haul did not replace its lost outlets. Today Ryder has 50 percent of the do-it-yourself moving market, helped in part by the demise of U-Haul's rental outlets.

I knew someone who worked for a heavy equipment supplier that paid its salespeople on commission. The company then decided that its salespeople were making too much money and put the salesforce on a salary plus bonus. Within the year, the once-successful company was out of business. Again, the company hadn't kept its placement strategy strong.

A&P was once the nation's leading retailer. Then it started to struggle. One of A&P's moves was to close unprofitable stores throughout the country. But that move sent a message to customers that A&P wasn't a winner, and A&P's successful stores started to struggle.

Interestingly enough, many of the A&Ps in Philadelphia were closed and then reopened under the Super Fresh name. The stores' new look avoided A&P's losing image and are now thriving. A&P's name change was a wise move and it helped rekindle A&P's marketing momentum. The A&P store by my home was instead taken over by Thriftway and is also doing well. Again, the store just needed a fresh face.

Will You Be in Business Forever?

Customers are risk averse when making a purchase. They want to be sure you're going to stay in business. For example, a mattress shop opened up in a nearby shopping center. It was a small store without much inventory, and it closed after three months. At the same time, another much larger mattress store opened. It appeared well financed and successful to customers.

I constantly see similar examples in retail stores, professional practices, and manufacturing companies. A business can't build momentum if people are worried about its future. I remember one time my wife and I went to a store to look at a new suit. I didn't buy there because the store had a handmade sign in the window announcing a sale. I wasn't about to buy a suit from a store that could afford only handmade signs.

Remember that every little detail of your business reflects an attitude to your customers. Make sure your business projects a successful image.

GENERAL MOTORS

When I was growing up, people used to say, "What's good for GM is good for the country." Now GM is operating without a profit and announcing plant closings.

We are witnessing the demise of what was once America's leading company. GM's downfall can be partially, if not totally, blamed on GM's failure to follow survival marketing tactics. Here is a list of some of the survival tactics GM has ignored:

Keep your prices at a level that will generate profits. GM ran a rebate program in the mid-80s to increase sales, but its competitors quickly followed with their own rebate programs. GM is still giving out rebates and still not making money.

Know the sales volume needed to survive. GM needs a high sales volume to cover its overhead. But in the late 1970s, GM standardized its product line to reduce production costs without initiating a program to compensate for the sales decline this move created.

Keep your products differentiated. GM's surge to the top of the automotive market was due to product differentiation between Chevrolets, Pontiacs, Buicks, and Oldsmobiles. If any company should have realized the importance of differentiation, it should have been GM.

Keep quality high. GM has let its quality reputation slide so far that *Consumer Reports* (April 1988, page 235) states that "new models from GM are likely to be troublesome."

Promote an important point. Chevrolet's "Heartbeat of America" campaign is meaningless. It says nothing about the car or the company.

Have a strong positioning strategy. GM's earlier strategy of providing cars for every market segment was effective. It projected the image that GM knew cars. But over the last five years, GM has not entered the new markets that have developed. The upscale sedan market is dominated by Volvo, BMW, and Audi. Chrysler dominates the minivan market which GM has entered but has been uncompetitive.

Keep your lead product strong. GM hasn't had a lead product strategy since the mid-1980s when it extensively promoted its Chevrolet Celebrity and the Oldsmobile Cutlass.

Keep your distribution strong. I recently purchased a car from Chrysler at a dealership that had the same owner as the Chevrolet dealership next door. When I asked why the owner had opened two dealerships, the salesman said it was because Chevrolet sales were too low to cover overhead expenses. Now the dealer splits his efforts between Chevrolet and Chrysler.

Know where your business will come from. Over the last three years, Ford and Chrysler have been introducing new cars, BMW and Volvo have been increasing sales, and the Japanese have been introducing family sedans—the heart of GM's business. Just where did GM think it was going to get more business? It certainly didn't develop a program to neutralize competition.

I don't think GM will ever recover its former market position; in fact, I think GM will continue to grow smaller as consumers lose confidence in the company's ability to build cars.

THE SEVEN-UP CO.

The Seven-Up Co. is a last example of a company not using survival tactics by failing to establish a defensible market position. Seven-Up's position is different than GM's because it has never been the market leader. But Seven-Up still should have been able to establish a defensible position. I'll examine where Seven-Up left itself vulnerable and then discuss what it could have done to strengthen its market position. Consider, first, Seven-Up's marketing situation:

Pepsi and Coke are both much larger than 7UP, and they dominate both promotional advertising and distribution outlets.

Most people drink a 7Up at least a few times during the year.

7UP has strong name recognition.

7UP is well differentiated as an alternative to colas.

For years 7UP was satisfied being the "uncola" and didn't mind if customers drank five colas for every 7UP. Seven-Up also had success with its distribution outlets; they too wanted to have an alternative to colas on the shelf.

But Seven-Up's strategy was missing some key defensive elements:

7UP was never promoted for its own taste. Consequently, it never developed a loyal customer base. In contrast, Dr Pepper developed a small, loyal group of customers that preferred Dr Pepper to all other drinks.

Seven-Up never tried to overcome its lack of control over its distribution network. It simply got by because of 7UP's name recognition and the limited number of cola alternatives.

7UP sales did well as long as the soft drink market grew. But when market growth slowed, Coke and Pepsi looked for ways to increase sales. Since 7UP was simply an alternative to colas, it was an easy target. Coke introduced Sprite, and Pepsi introduced Slice. Now the big two will start to use their distribution muscle to ease 7UP off of supermarket shelves.

Seven-Up needed a more defensible program when its sales were strong. It needed to communicate to customers:

- 7UP was an alternative to colas
- When it was time not to drink a cola
- Why 7UP was the perfect drink for those times

Seven-Up's program should have had a theme more along the line of "It's 7UP time." Such a theme would have established when and why a customer should drink 7UP and would have created a more loyal customer base.

Seven-Up's program also needed a better placement strategy. It might have considered joining with RC Cola, A&W Root Beer, Orange Crush, and Dr Pepper to compete more effectively for space in distribution outlets.

SUMMARY

I used the examples of General Motors and Seven-Up Co. because I want to emphasize that you can't wait until trouble starts to think about survival tactics. You need to think about them every time you do a marketing program.

CHAPTER 6

WHAT'S HAPPENING NOW?

A clothing store's sales have dropped 15 percent over the last year, and now it has to get sales back up or it will close. The clothing store has an immediate crisis. Other examples of "what's happening now" scenarios are:

A new tax law places extra reporting requirements on businesses. Accountants offer opportunities to obtain new clients and to increase billings with existing clients.

An industry starts to change technology. A supplier to the industry wants to reposition itself as a "partner in industry progress" to gain market share.

A hotel's chief competitor just dropped prices 25 percent. The hotel needs an action plan to hold market share and profitability.

The issues covered in Chapters 2–5 are important for strategic, long-term business growth. What's-happening issues deal with situations that need to be resolved today.

I'm covering what's-happening issues last for the simple reason that most marketing strategies deal only with these issues. They completely neglect the important strategic moves needed for long-term growth. Typical marketing plans call for matching competitive price cuts, printing new literature, running an ad campaign, and maybe getting more distributors. You should consider both short- and long-term issues in your marketing plans. I've put what's-happening issues last to be sure you don't forget to include long-term marketing tactics in your plans—or better yet, to help you solve short-term problems with long-term solutions.

This chapter has three sections:

1. Sales and market share trends: how to use sales trends to determine your current problems.
2. Current problems and opportunities: how to examine problems and opportunities to create a long-term marketing strategy that also resolves an immediate crisis.
3. What competitors will do next: how to anticipate what programs or products competitors might be ready to introduce.

SALES AND MARKET SHARE TRENDS

Your Sales History

Look critically at your sales history over the last three years, and determine why sales are up, down, or flat. A common mistake marketers make is to do a cursory analysis of historical sales. Past sales and the reasons why sales are growing or declining can often pinpoint real problems.

As an example, consider an outlet specializing in clothes for teens that opened three years ago. The first year, sales were strong; but since then, sales have dropped 10 percent per year.

The store manager thought sales were dropping because teens were buying fewer clothes. The manager had checked with a women's fashion outlet next door and found it had steady sales over the last three years. Since the manager hadn't changed the store since it opened, his quick analysis was that teens just weren't buying as many clothes as they did when the store opened.

The store manager's analysis was too fast. The store had about 15 teenage employees who thought the reason for the store's sales decline was that the store's prices, though lower than normal retail prices, were not as low as sales prices at a nearby mall. The employees felt customers were shopping at the mall before coming to the outlet. The manager started watching sales ads and found out the employees were right.

The manager therefore cut back on his number of promotions and offered instead to match sales prices of mall stores. Business picked back up.

Review your sales data, and list all the significant events that occurred that affected sales. List also the events that you thought might impact sales but didn't. As an example, I'll look at the sales history for a dental delivery unit I once marketed (the unit that supplies the air and water a high-speed drill needs).

Delivery Unit Sales History	Significant Events
Year 1: 800 units	A major competitor's promotion offered an incentive sales trip contest for dealer salespeople. We ran a package discount program on our delivery units. A small competitor doubled sales due to its high-quality product.
Year 2: 1,000 units	. We introduced a new dental chair. A major competitor introduced a new delivery unit. No major promotions were introduced by any competitor.
Year 3: 700 units	We ran a dealer sales contest. The small, high quality competitor took our #3 market share position. A dental chair competitor introduced a new product which hurt sales of our entire product line.

Dental chairs were our lead product; we felt our sales history indicated that delivery unit sales were pulled by chair sales. The immediate problem was that we were losing delivery unit sales due to a competitor's dental chair introduction. We switched to a package promotion, offering dealers an incentive to purchase dental chair/delivery unit combinations. Packaging the two products raised delivery unit sales about 20 percent.

The purpose of studying sales history is, first, to see what programs might work best and, second, to see what competitive events might hurt sales the most. In the delivery unit example, any program that would link delivery unit sales to chairs would increase sales, and any new competitive dental chair would hurt sales.

Market Share Trends

Market share trends are helpful, especially when a market is growing or shrinking. For example, in a rapidly growing market, a manufacturer might have rapidly increasing sales and still be losing market share— an indication to the manufacturer that its market position is weakening. Or if a market is declining, a manufacturer may be increasing its market share while its sales are dropping.

Market share data helps supplement sales data to give you a better idea of your marketing performance. For example, I'll consider two scenarios for the dental delivery unit.

	Scenario 1		
	Total Market Units	Co. Units	Market Share
Year 1 sales	10,000	800	8.0%
Year 2 sales	12,000	1,000	8.3%
Year 3 sales	9,000	700	7.8%
	Scenario 2		
	Total Market Units	Co. Units	Market Share
Year 1 sales	10,000	800	8.0%
Year 2 sales	10,000	1,000	10.0%
Year 3 sales	8,500	700	8.2%

It would be difficult to draw any firm conclusions from scenario 1 because of the small percentage changes in market share. The drop in market share in year 3 could have been due to the emergence of the small competitor with quality products or to the introduction of a competitive dental chair. The market share rise in year 2 could be attributed to the absence of a major competitive promotion or to our introduction of a dental chair.

Scenario 2, however, makes the relationship between dental chair and delivery unit sales clearer. The similar market share change, both up and down, appears to tie into the introduction of first ours and then our competitor's dental chair.

If you compare market share trends for all major competitors, the market trends can become crystal clear. I'll consider a market trend chart for the four significant competitors in the market:

1. Competitor A: delivery unit market leader; only sells delivery units.

    2. Competitor B: co-leader in dental chair market; also sells delivery units; introduced chair in year 3.

    3. Competitor C: my company; co-leader in dental chair market; supplements chair sales with delivery units; introduced dental chair in year 2.

    4. Competitor D: emerging competitor with a high-quality unit; does not sell other products.

Delivery Units—Market Share Trends

	Market Shares		
	Year 1	*Year 2*	*Year 3*
Competitor A	46.0%	45.5%	45.0%
Competitor B	16.8	13.7	15.7
Competitor C	8.0	10.0	8.2
Competitor D	4.5	6.5	8.5
Others	24.7	24.3	22.6

    This chart indicates the following things: the relationship between dental chairs and delivery units for both competitors B and C and the fact that customers appreciate competitor D's quality approach.

    Market share data is difficult for most companies to get, especially when they have only two or three local competitors. This often tempts marketers to overlook market share trends; however, that's a mistake. If you overlook market share trends, you'll miss some vital clues that help explain your current marketing situation.

    With a little creativity, most businesses can get an idea if their market share is rising or falling. The following examples show how you can use your ingenuity.

1. 7-Eleven

A 7-Eleven was the only convenience food store in a town of 5,000 until six months ago when a WaWa store opened. 7-Eleven's volume dropped 30 percent, but the owner wasn't sure how her volume compared to WaWa's. To compare sales volume, the owner:

    Compared locations. Both stores were centrally located in the town and had about the same amount of street traffic.

Compared the number of people who went into each store over six similar one-hour periods. Again, each store had close to the same number of customers.

The store manager believed the two stores had equal market shares. She also decided to monitor both stores' traffic every three months.

2. Home Elevators
The president of a manufacturing company selling home elevators took the following steps to determine his market share:

Requested the annual reports of his publicly owned competitors through his stockbroker.

Phoned public libraries in the hometowns of privately held competitors and asked if they had a directory of area companies that listed sales volume and/or number of employees.

Started a log tracking elevator bids. Each elevator manufacturer had installers in each state. When an architect designed a home with an elevator, he or she would send out bids to two to five installers. The sales department logged in each bid and later added the company that was awarded the bid.

CURRENT PROBLEMS AND OPPORTUNITIES

Problems

Current and upcoming products are the heart of most marketing plans. They are issues that must be addressed to keep a company's momentum high. The key to a successful marketing program is creating plans that both solve short-term problems and create long-term marketing benefits.

You need to follow a three-step process to develop a winning marketing program.

1. Discover the marketing elements that make a product successful.
2. Determine what marketing elements are hampering a product's success.
3. Evaluate how current problems and opportunities can be addressed with one or more of a product's key marketing elements.

As an example of the three-step process, I'll track the marketing planning process of Sue, the manager of a motel on an interstate exit, whose major competitor just dropped its prices 20 percent.

Sue's first inclination was to drop her prices from $48.00 to $38.00, which would be $3.00 higher than the competitor's price. Sue's motel is a little nicer and better known to justify a $3.00 premium. But Sue was worried the motel couldn't be profitable at $38.00 per night, so she decided to put aside her initial panic and go through the three-step planning process.

Step 1: Discover key marketing elements that make a product successful.
   • Sue's motel was the closest motel to a nearby large industrial center.
   • Forty percent of Sue's clients were businesspeople who were repeat customers.

Step 2: Determine what marketing elements are hindering a product's success.
   • The two closest exits to Sue had three motels each. Those two exits were located at the area's two busiest highways. All six competitors have higher occupancy rates than Sue's motel.
   • Sue's motel was poorly differentiated from competitors' motels.
   • Few family vacationers stayed at Sue's motel.

Step 3: Evaluate how current problems and opportunities can be addressed with one or more of a product's key marketing elements.
   • Sue decided to imitate the strategy of a motel she stayed at during her last vacation that would utilize her key marketing elements. Sue's moves would also differentiate the motel from her competitors'.
   • Forty percent of the rooms were set up as business traveler suites. One double bed was removed and replaced with a table and two chairs. Each room also had its own coffee pot. This move capitalized on Sue's past success with business travelers.
   • Ten percent of the rooms were converted to kitchenettes. They had a small refrigerator, two-burner countertop stove, small sink, and two cupboards. This step addressed the motel's weakness with family vacationers.

Sue did drop her prices for 30 days until she could obtain financing to start the remodeling process. But after 30 days, Sue had some of the rooms remodeled and was able to return to her original pricing.

There are two interesting points about this example. First, Sue probably knew for a few years that she needed to make changes in her motel, but she didn't get around to it until she was forced to by a competitor. It's hard to make changes when sales are going well. But if your marketing program isn't constantly improving the company's position, sooner or later you will end up with a severe marketing problem like Sue's.

Second, Sue knew of a motel with a strong strategy. She had probably determined, before the competitor's price action, that this strategy would work at her motel. I think every marketer should keep a file of potential strategies to refer to when creating a marketing plan.

Opportunities

Invariably, every market has some opportunities developing. Opportunities present a difficult challenge to marketers. On the one hand, you don't want to miss an opportunity and surrender momentum to competitors. An example is Xerox and the way it failed to enter the market for small copiers. On the other hand, you don't want to rush into a market and not have a defensible strategy. An example is Texas Instruments and the way it entered the personal computer market with a "me too" product; it was forced to drop out of the market in less than two years.

There are two strategies involved with opportunities: first, establish market presence and, second, establish a defensible position.

When an opportunity is just coming onto the horizon, you should do something to make the market aware that you are interested. Often you can do this without committing to a major program. Examples of developing a market presence are:

An active public relations campaign announces a crash development program for a personal computer.

An accountant runs a series of seminars explaining the new tax laws before his program is ready to handle new tax reporting requirements.

A manufacturer distributes a product in the new market from an overseas supplier.

Top management sets up meetings with company officials in the new market to explore what products are needed.

Engineers become involved in the new technical societies revolving around the new market.

A manufacturer modifies an existing product so that it is applicable for a segment of the new market.

A retailer opens three trial stores in one city to explore the market potential of the new market opportunity.

A retailer rents a pushcart in a mall with the new product prior to reconfiguring his store to handle the new merchandise.

Top management runs a publicized market survey on what features a new product should have.

You have three goals in establishing market awareness. First, it makes potential customers aware that you might be introducing a product. Second, it alerts potential competitors that you will be in the market, possibly delaying their market entry. And third, it provides you with more complete feedback about the new opportunity and the extent of its sales potential.

The second phase of action for new market opportunities is to establish a defensible position. Many marketers find it hard to think about defensible strategies when they are on the leading edge of a new market development; they anticipate only the seemingly unlimited sales possibilities.

For example, a few years ago, fiber optic connectors represented a new market opportunity for connector companies. The first products were introduced by small connector manufacturers whose sales growth was phenomenal. Each manufacturer was doing all it could to meet the demands for new connectors. Then AMP, the market leader in connectors, entered the market with a broad product line, eventually forcing most of the small companies out of business. The small companies needed to find a market niche to specialize in or to devise another tactic that would create a defensible market position.

Because the potential of new opportunities is usually not clear, I prefer a two-step approach in dealing with them. First, create market awareness, a step that helps you be prepared if the opportunity is significant, and helps you decide if an opportunity is worth pursuing. Once you determine a market is worth entering, develop a defensible strategy.

WHAT WILL YOUR COMPETITORS DO NEXT?

Most companies will, at some interval, introduce a new product or marketing program. For example, Pepsi has a new promotional program about every six months, and Ford tries to introduce a new car every two years. It's wise to track all of your competitors' moves. You want to be prepared when a competitor launches a new product or program.

For example, Rossignol, a ski manufacturer, has four major competitors. This is what its competitive action chart might look like:

Competitor Action Chart—Rossignol Ski Manufacturer

	Marketing Programs		Product Introductions	
	Intervals	Due Date	Intervals	Due Date
Competitor A	every Nov.	Nov. 89	2 years	Nov. 90
Competitor B	every Nov.	Nov. 89	3 years	Nov. 90
Competitor C	every Nov.	Nov. 89	2 years	Nov. 89
Competitor D	every Oct.	Oct. 89	3 years	Oct. 91

If your competitors are due to release a product or program, you should be ready in order to keep up your marketing momentum. Try to run big programs shortly before a competitor does, and most of all, try to avoid getting complacent when sales are up.

PART 1 SUMMARY

RATE YOUR PRODUCT AGAINST COMPETITION

The last step in analyzing your business is to rate your product, store, or service against the competition's. You may have a poor marketing position, but luckily, so do your competitors—or, every competitor may be marketing effectively. Rating yourself against your competitors helps you determine how urgent it is to improve your marketing position. If your rating is far below competition, you need to immediately start a strong marketing program. I'll use the Denny's family restaurant in my neighborhood as an example of how to rate your product. A brief description of Denny's and its four competitors follows:

> Denny's: a family-style restaurant with a poorly differentiated menu; has the poorest location of any of the competitors; benefits from national advertising and the large number of Denny's restaurants in the northern suburbs of Philadelphia.
>
> Bob's Big Boy: a family restaurant; features "all you can eat" nights; located on the busiest intersection in the area.
>
> Friendly's: features ice cream desserts; location in a large mall; well-known restaurant chain in Philadelphia.
>
> The Ground Round: features free popcorn and old children's movies; caters to families with young children.
>
> Valley Forge Diner: local diner with an extensive menu; appeals primarily to singles and couples; serves a variety of regional dishes; excellent location on a busy highway.

Denny's certainly has areas that need improving, especially in the area of product differentiation, but Denny's is not in immediate

FIGURE 6-1
Denny's Rating versus Competition

	Denny's versus Bob's Big Boy	Denny's versus Friendly's	Denny's versus The Ground Round	Denny's versus Valley Forge Diner
1. Quality	3	2	3	3
2. Service	3	2	3	4
3. Name recognition	2	3	2	2
4. Price/value relationship	3	4	4	3
5. Product features	3	3	3	3
6. Product differentiation	4	4	4	4
7. Placement strategy (location)	4	4	4	4
8. Market share	3	2	2	2
9. Promotion expenditures	2	3	2	1
10. Financial strength	3	3	3	2
11. Defensibility of market position	3	3	2	3
Average score	3	2.8	2.9	2.8

Rating scale: 1 = Much better   2 = Better   3 = About the same   4 = Worse   5 = Much worse trouble. Its strong name recognition, high market share, and promotional spending currently are keeping it competitive. By the way, Denny's high market share exists primarily because of its strong breakfast business; The Ground Round does not offer breakfast, and Friendly's serves a late breakfast due to its mall location.

In your own analysis, include a rating of your versus you competitors' salesforces if it is important to your product's success. I didn't include it in Denny's example because it didn't apply. Also, include in the rating any other marketing element that may be important to your business.

If your ratings show that you are going head to head against a much stronger competitor, you should look for a market niche you can excel in. The odds are against a small competitor displacing a large, well-entrenched competitor. An example is the way Heinz and Campbell's occasionally go after each other's market. Despite heavy expenditures, Campbell's still holds on to its number one soup market share, and Heinz still dominates the ketchup market.

Instead of trying to dislodge a large competitor, try instead to find a small market opening. Lipton did this successfully with its "cup of soup" products. Instead of introducing soup in a can like Campbell's, Lipton offered a serving of powdered soup in a package.

Before turning to Chapter 7, make a list of the key marketing elements for your business. You will need to refer to the list as you continue to create your marketing plan.

PART 2

CHOOSING AND IMPLEMENTING A WINNING MARKETING STRATEGY

Choosing a marketing strategy is the most difficult part of a marketing plan. At times I've considered a dozen possible strategies before finding the right one. Chapter 7 provides guidelines for using your intuitive knowledge of your customers and products to create an effective strategy. But don't simply choose the first strategy you think of. Instead, create four or five sound strategies, and select the best one. My experience is that improving a strategy 10 percent will increase sales 30 to 50 percent. So it is wise to spend a little extra time to develop an effective strategy.

Chapter 8 covers the tactics you can use to effectively communicate your new marketing message. I've found that many companies simply do not know how to pick the right implementation tactics. Too often companies use whatever tactics they are familiar with or whatever tactics a salesperson has just sold them. This chapter is designed to put you in control of your implementation tactics, allowing you to determine which ones are best for your product and customers.

Chapter 9 explains the concept of inside-out marketing. The title of this book is *Total Marketing* because an effective marketing program considers every aspect of your business. Inside-out marketing explains how a marketer can use every aspect of his or her business to add to the company's marketing effort.

Before you can start choosing a marketing strategy, you need to decide what the objectives are for your business. Without an objective you won't be able to evaluate which strategies will work best.

As an example, I'll consider my father's drugstore. At the age of 58, his objective was to double his retirement fund before he turned 65. Earning enough to increase his fund was difficult because the drugstore was in a declining neighborhood. His strategy was to strengthen his relationship with two nursing homes by adding two services the nursing homes requested and visiting each home at least once a week. My father was also careful to target two smaller nursing homes to minimize competition from the big drug chains.

If a younger pharmacist had owned the store, he might have had an objective to expand business and open up two or three new stores. The nursing home strategy wouldn't provide enough income for this pharmacist. He would need instead a strategy to attract people from outside the neighborhood to the store. Or he might need to consider moving the store to a growing neighborhood.

Objectives are usually a matter of personal choice rather than a business decision. They are primarily based upon the amount of money, time, risk, and effort a person or company is willing to commit to a product.

Setting objectives for a marketing plan requires you to:

• Decide on long-term objectives.
• Choose objectives for the next year.
• Evaluate those objectives against the market situation and the resources available.
• Determine what objectives can be reached over the next year.

A marketing plan is a dynamic process. You need give and take between what you would like to accomplish and what you have the resources to accomplish. I've often gone through three or four strategies before I found one that best utilizes the available resources.

You may find that your objectives are not possible with the current market conditions. Then you need to either change your objectives or find another business.

Chapter 7

CHOOSING A
MARKETING THRUST

What's the message you want to send to the market this year? What do you want prospects to remember? How are you going to get customers to purchase your product? Your next step in creating a marketing plan is choosing a thrust that focuses on a key marketing element.

After reading the last six chapters, you should have several key marketing elements in mind for your marketing thrust. If you own a clothing store in a mall, you might decide that your store has poor name recognition, is poorly differentiated from the competition, or has the wrong pricing structure for its image. Or if you're a consultant, you may feel that you are not presenting enough proposals, and when you do, your closing rate is low.

Early in the planning cycle, most marketers have a tendency to focus on just one critical area. The clothing store owner might concentrate exclusively on pricing strategy. This could be a mistake. It might turn out that she can't afford to change prices without destroying profit margins. Thus, the owner should consider a thrust for each identified problem until she is certain that one thrust will work. A checklist at the end of this chapter will help you determine if a particular thrust can be successfully implemented.

The goal of this chapter is to help you develop your own marketing thrust. To do this, the chapter is full of examples which might relate to your business. The examples are divided into six sections.

1. Building off strengths.
2. Building off successful campaigns.
3. Compensating for or correcting problems.
4. Effective marketing thrusts.

5. Poor marketing thrusts.
6. Difficult marketing problems.

At the end of the chapter, I'll use the marketing thrust checklist to choose among six possible thrusts for Hitachi VCRs.

BUILDING OFF STRENGTHS

Building off a strength that customers recognize is an excellent way to create a marketing thrust. Mercedes-Benz builds off its quality image with a program advertising its top-of-the-line cars. Another successful program is K mart's blue-light specials. K mart makes it a point to have blue-light specials every half hour. This is a major thrust and certainly contributes to its position as a discount store. My father's drugstore is in an old neighborhood. His store is popular with the older people who have shopped there for years. To capitalize on his popularity with senior citizens, he replaced the toy department with a consignment boutique of handcrafts made by many of his customers.

Examples of building on strengths are:

A shoe store which primarily sells athletic footwear might have professional athletes sign autographs in the store once a month.

A popular party paper goods store could redecorate its front windows every two weeks.

A wallpaper store which specializes in having a wide variety of wallpaper books could have a large sign in the window to keep people informed of the new books in stock.

A grocery store known for its excellent meat selection could add a special department for unusual meats for different seasons.

Whenever possible, capitalize on an image people already have of you. The Xerox commercial "We are as good as a Xerox" is a good example of capitalizing on a product's perceived superiority.

Not all of your strengths lie in the public's perception of a product. Your greatest strength may be in your distribution channel. You might want to implement marketing programs aimed at retail salespeople. An example of this tactic is offering a trip for two to Europe to salespeople who obtain a certain sales volume. Or you may want to offer a co-op advertising program. In a typical co-op program, a manufacturer sets up an advertising fund for each distributor or retailer equal to 1 or 2 percent of its purchases. The retailer can use the fund to pay for up to half of any ad campaign that promotes the manufacturer's products. In the most successful distributor program I've seen, the manufacturer offered to build in-store displays for its retailers, as long as only the manufacturer's products were placed on it.

All of the programs mentioned so far involve building off strengths the customer knows you have, but sometimes you have strengths customers don't know about. For example, Pepsi's taste test campaign emphasized what Pepsi thought was an unknown strength—taste superiority over Coke. Features/benefits programs showing how a product outperforms another can also focus on an unknown strength.

You can also run a standard features/benefits ad to introduce a new strength. One product I marketed advertised a revolutionary feature, but follow-up market surveys indicated that people didn't care about that feature. Instead, they were buying the product because they thought it had high quality. We quickly changed our ad campaign to stress the product's high quality.

If you have certain strengths, don't dilute your message by trying to say too much. People really don't absorb a lot of information from any company's campaign. They will remember, at best, three items. As you introduce more information into a campaign, you reduce the chances of a customer remembering it. Take your main points and hit them hard. It is for this reason I love a new campaign I've seen for an RCA video camera. It focuses on a father taping his three-year-old. The ad had only one point—that anyone can make a high-quality video tape with an RCA video camera.

BUILDING OFF SUCCESSFUL CAMPAIGNS
OF THE PAST

Some marketing programs are popular with customers. If you have a program which was popular in the past, build future programs around it. For example, Miller Lite continues to use its original concept of pro athletes in commercials. Pepsi has successfully used its theme of a "Taste for a New Generation" for three or four years.

Other examples of continuing themes are United Airlines' "Fly the Friendly Skies" and Budweiser's "King of Beers." I also like the way

Budweiser continually uses the Clydesdales. Wisk had done well for a long time with "Ring Around the Collar." Campaigns don't have to be repeats of earlier programs to give them continuity. McDonald's runs many programs geared to children. When McDonald's promoted its Happy Meals, it was continuing its children-oriented theme.

If you are focusing your campaign at the point of distribution and want push versus pull marketing, you also can repeat successful programs. For example, if one set of sales promotion materials worked well, you may want to introduce similar materials the next year. It can be effective to have distributors run major campaigns on a different product of your line each year. If you are focusing on the distributors, you really must be consistent. You can't run a pull program directed at the consumers one year, followed by a push program through your distributors the next. Distributors like to stock two or three major brands, and they won't make your product one of these if they don't know what to expect from you from one year to the next.

One of the major advantages of staying with a continuing theme is that customers come to recognize it as yours; after all, you may have been using it for several years. Don't change campaigns unless you think the new program will be at least 20 percent more effective than the old program. It's just too difficult to communicate with the market. You will get bored with a particular campaign long before your customers will.

Before continuing, I would like to comment on what might seem to be contradictory themes. In the last six chapters, I dwelled on continually looking for areas in which your company could be improved. Now I'm telling you to stay with successful programs. But these two ideas aren't contradictory. In many cases, you may have a good thrust or concentration of effort already existing in your business. What your business evaluation may have pointed out are items which prevent you from completing your marketing thrust. For example, let's look at a hardware store which has a large inventory. Its inventory has been advertised for years, and people know the store is well stocked. The only problem is that the store doesn't have enough experienced staff; no one ever knows where to find things. You can easily meld these factors into a solid thrust for the next year. First, you could initiate a training program so every clerk would know where items are located. Then you could advertise that not only does the store have everything, but a customer can find it, buy it, and leave within five minutes.

Or consider a drugstore which caters to older people; it might need better delivery service. A party goods store may find that people don't really know how many different items they need for a party. The store could assemble party packages. It could have as a thrust its expanded party goods capability. A wallpaper store may find that its customers are overwhelmed by too many choices, so it could rearrange wallpaper selections into different style types, such as early American and contemporary.

COMPENSATING FOR OR CORRECTING PROBLEMS

Maybe you have decided that your current marketing programs and strategies aren't working. You therefore want to initiate a new campaign.

One example of correction thrust was AMC's campaign to re-establish Renault as a quality car; it featured George C. Scott to give the product credibility. And earlier in the 1980s was Ford's thrust "Quality is Job One." These companies decided to change their marketing thrust when they discovered a problem area in their business evaluation.

A major change in thrust does not mean changing everything in your strategy. For example, consider a grocery store with the best meat in the area. Originally it was an A&P store that closed because it was about a third the size of other grocery stores; it couldn't stock enough inventory. When Thriftway moved into the spot, it had the same problems until the store decided to differentiate itself by concentrating on the meat department.

Other thrust changes may be more subtle. Cadillac used to run commercials promoting its features and benefits. In 1986 those commercials were abandoned when all Cadillac commercials were run by local dealers. The company stopped its own ads, and promoted itself instead with a co-op advertising program. Most consumers probably didn't notice this change; the same message was being conveyed. But Cadillac had decided to advertise regionally through its dealers rather than nationally.

Another subtle thrust change was made when General Electric introduced a program which stressed how its appliances could be serviced at home by a homemaker. A last example is an outlet store in my area that added employees whose sole function was to put clothes back on the racks. Now in both cases, the companies were correcting a problem area, but General Electric and the discount store kept the same image.

General Electric is still a consumer goods company, and the outlet store is still an outlet store. But the changes, although not dramatic, added effectively to their established positions.

In many competitive markets, a difference in marketing effectiveness of only 5 to 10 percent can determine success or failure. Enhancing an established position can often be your best thrust. For example, Seven-Up ran its "uncola" program for years. This was followed by "No caffeine, Never had it, Never will." The continuity of the two programs proved so successful that the competitors were forced to introduce caffeine-free sodas.

If, on the other hand, you decide on a major repositioning strategy, you will lose some of the effectiveness of earlier programs. For years Burger King's program was "Have it your way," an effective positioning slogan. Then Burger King switched to the slogan "Fast food for fast times." These two programs are almost complete opposites. One promises that Burger King will take the time to let you have it your way. The other promises your food as fast as possible. It's often difficult to recover the momentum lost when radically changing positioning strategies.

However, a totally new marketing direction can be effective. Stroh's Beer successfully changed its campaign theme from "fire-brewed beer" to one in which Alex the dog loves the taste of Stroh's. Dairy Queen, in the Midwest, successfully changed its focus from ice cream store to full-service restaurant. And Great Adventure amusement park in New Jersey increased its business when the marketing emphasis was switched from thrilling rides to family entertainment.

Jeep is another company that successfully changed directions. Up to the mid-1970s, Jeep was a tough, off-the-road vehicle with a spartan interior. Jeep was far and away the market leader in off-the-road vehicles, but that market segment was shrinking. So Jeep was reintroduced as a family vehicle that happened to have four-wheel drive. Jeep's sales increased with this strategy, and now Jeep is extremely profitable.

If you have decided that a marketing thrust must be changed, list all of the changes and improvements you noted while reading Chapters 2–6, and try to group them into categories. You should then decide which area needs to be changed quickest. There are two considerations: What changes can help the most, and what is the cost of these changes? Don't choose a program that's too expensive to properly execute. The checklist at the end of this chapter will help you pick a thrust you can execute.

EFFECTIVE MARKETING THRUSTS

1. Cadillac

Cadillac has done an outstanding marketing job in reorienting its program toward its dealers. The marketers at Cadillac had a serious problem. Cadillac had taken its nice, old, conservative, and highly differentiated car and made it look like an Oldsmobile—and, at $10,000 more. True, Cadillac was previously purchased primarily by older people, and yes, it had an image problem. But to make it look like an Oldsmobile was foolish.

Cadillac marketers recognized their mistake and did not want to show their new model on TV, telling everyone how great it was. There was no point in trying to fool the public by saying that the Cadillac was still a well-differentiated product. Instead marketers gave promotion money to local dealers to they could run programs that would be effective in their local areas. I don't know how Cadillac sales are doing, but using push marketing through its dealers was a smart decision in face of a poor product decision.

2. Ford

Ford has had two major thrusts over the last few years. The first is "Quality is Job One," and the second is that Ford builds cars "with the shape of things to come." In other words, Ford is building cars which are ahead of its time, and Ford is an innovator. In both instances, Ford gives the impression that it is a company that really knows the car business. These thrusts are simple, meaningful, and effective.

3. Dean Witter

I really like Dean Witter's campaign "You're somebody at Dean Witter." The program augments Dean Witter's connection to the little guy through its ties with Sears. Other brokerage houses like E. F. Hutton come across as intimidating, caring only about the big investors. Both E. F. Hutton's campaigns, "When E. F. Hutton talks, people listen" and the Bill Cosby spots, imply that E. F. Hutton is looking for the big investor. Dean Witter's campaign is based on being a friend to the little guy. It operates that same way.

4. Michelin Tires

Michelin runs a program with babies playing happily amongst tires with the theme "Because so much is riding on your tires." Michelin is a known name, and its tires are considered to be outstanding, though expensive. Michelin's problem is convincing people that its tires are worth the extra money. Its campaign is much better than a features/benefits ad because the campaign deals with the emotion of purchasing a premium product.

5. Pepsi

Pepsi has done a great job positioning itself as the drink for younger people. First it promoted the taste tests in which Pepsi claimed its taste was better than that of the traditional market leader Coke. The new Pepsi campaign, "Choice of the new generation," builds wonderfully on that same concept. Of course, Coke helped Pepsi by switching over to a product with a "Pepsi" taste. Building on a strong concept is an excellent strategy, and Pepsi does it well.

6. Prudential

For the past 20 years, Prudential has used a strong visual image: "The rock." This is an excellent image for an insurance company: solid, dependable, and consistent. Other good examples of companies with memorable visual images are Walt Disney's Mickey Mouse and Budweiser's Clydesdales.

7. Party Time USA

This party supply store is in my neighborhood. The first thing I like about the store is that it has a big sign; you can't miss it. Next, it is in a building that was formerly a factory or warehouse; the store looks like an outlet. Also, the windows always have attractive seasonal displays. Now comes my favorite part of Party Time USA's marketing program: It has shopping carts. Shopping carts to pick up some paper plates and cups? Nooo! Those carts just put you in the frame of mind to buy a lot. I always purchase two or three times what I think I should because of those darn carts. The store is segmented nicely, too. One area has complete packages of everything you need for any party event. Other areas are segregated by price: top of the line, mid-range, and economy. That's the type of total marketing approach I like to see.

8. Lee's Hoagies

I live in the Philadelphia area where hoagies and cheese steaks are popular. Most hoagie places are somewhat grimy, and they rarely look attractive from the outside. Lee's Hoagies is different. Besides having a big, noticeable sign, the shop looks like a fun place to eat. It has a beautiful serving counter. The sandwich ingredients, which always look fresh, are in display cases where you can see them. But what makes Lee's marketing program exceptional is that it has big store windows so passersby can look in and see how attractive everything looks.

9. Jiffy Lube

Now, I'm not sure about all Jiffy Lubes, but the one by my home has done an effective job of marketing. Because it is located in an old gas station, the first thing the owners did was to clean up the pavement and clean and remodel the station. In a clean waiting room, a host or hostess takes customer information. The image projected is that getting an oil change is a pleasant experience—much, much different from the local gas station. I get my oil changed at Jiffy Lube every 5,000 miles now. Before, I'm not sure I changed it more than once a year.

10. The Troubador Music Shop

This is a small store in my neighborhood, jammed with a wide variety of musical instruments. Now, the store itself is very small. It doesn't look like it would hold a large inventory, and it doesn't do much to grab your attention. But the owner does a simple thing that is effective marketing. Sometimes, when the weather is nice, he puts a few unusual items out on the sidewalk by his store. People walking by can't help but notice that this little bitty store has a lot of inventory.

I used the last examples for a reason. Effective marketing does not necessarily involve elaborate strategies; it can be accomplished by the simplest things. These ideas apply from the largest to the smallest company. I've always felt, for instance, that IBM's success was based largely upon its willingness to overcome customers' fear of computers by providing support people. That is a basic marketing strategy.

POOR MARKETING THRUSTS

1. RCA

RCA is active in three competitive markets: VCRs, VCR tapes, and VCR cameras. Now, there is one unusual factor here. RCA has a strong position in all three markets, while many other competitors don't. Having a package of products and services should give RCA an advantage, yet RCA has not exploited this edge. Missing golden opportunities is lousy marketing.

Recently I visited a local electronics retailer. In one part of the store, there was a large stack of RCA tapes on sale; in another, there was a large stack of RCA VCRs; and in another, there were RCA video cameras. I couldn't help but think how appealing it would have been to see the three products combined into an RCA display. The store could have been showing home videos of little kids on an RCA TV. It would have been excellent marketing for RCA, and I think the store would have liked the promotion because it would grab the customers' attention.

2. Coke

I'm not going to criticize Coke again for introducing new Coke. Consider, however, what Coke has done since that introduction. First, Coke changed the product's name to Classic Coke. This new name reinforced Pepsi's position as the "choice of a new generation." Young people—the new generation—are the very people Coke was trying to appeal to with new Coke.

Second, consider the outrage of the consumers when Coke dropped old Coca Cola. It may have been the biggest protest of the year. People didn't just like Coke—they were willing to take to the streets in protest to get old Coca Cola back. How could Coke pass up this opportunity for a tremendous marketing campaign? Now, I have a theory about soft drinks. After you drink a certain soft drink for a week or two, you become accustomed to the taste; another soft drink doesn't taste as good. I would have thought a campaign to have people try new Coke for a week or two was in order. But I don't think the Coke executives wanted to admit their mistake. I think they could have capitalized on it for some great publicity. As a rule, people will be supportive of a company that admits a marketing mistake.

3. The Paper Outlet

If you recall the section on good marketing examples, you will remember I wrote about Party Time USA. I thought I'd give an example of a similar store with a poor marketing thrust. The difference between the two stores to an untrained observer may be small, but the good marketing strategy of one store versus the poor strategy of the other can make the difference between success and failure. The Paper Outlet has a small sign, not big enough to create a positive impression. I also don't really like the name The Paper Outlet; it doesn't sound like a party goods store. Window displays have a hodgepodge look, and they are not memorable.

The store is located in a small shop in a shopping strip. Despite its name, it doesn't look like an outlet. It looks like it must be a specialty shop because the store is so small. Finally, the merchandise is poorly chosen, and it's all premium priced. The merchandise doesn't match the image of an outlet store.

4. *U.S. News and World Report*

U.S. News and World Report, a news magazine, ran a campaign with the slogan "Don't read us if you want to read about Madonna." (Madonna is a rock and roll singer.) Included in the ad was a picture of a *Time* magazine cover featuring Madonna. On one hand, this ad is commendable. It emphasizes that *U.S. News and World Report* is a news magazine. Every marketing thrust should strive to be this simple and direct.

So what's wrong with the program? It misrepresents a competitor. *Time* magazine contains 60 to 80 percent news. It does have stories about people like Madonna, but it is basically a news magazine. By misrepresenting *Time*, *U.S. News and World Report* is harming its credibility. It appears to be trying to deceive its audience, and trying to fool customers is always a bad tactic. It is especially bad when your target audience is informed professionals.

5. Hair Stylist

There is a hair cutting salon by my home that advertises low prices and no appointments. But there is one serious problem: there is always a one- to two-hour wait to get a haircut. What sense does this make? I'd rather make an appointment than wait two hours.

6. Philadelphia

I like living in the Philadelphia area because there is a tremendous variety of things to do. Yet the slogan Philadelphia uses to market itself is all wrong. It simply states, "Get to know us."

Philadelphia's problem is that its attractions are spread over a wide region. Outside of Independence Hall and the Liberty Bell, the attractions are not well known to most tourists. On top of that, the major hotels are not near popular historical sites. The result is that tourists stop over in Philadelphia for a two- or three-hour visit between stops to Atlantic City, New Jersey, and Lancaster, Pennsylvania. That's too little time to get to know an interesting city.

What Philadelphia needs is packaging; it needs to provide tourists with day-long itineraries. For example, the cultural programs, historical sites, country estates, examples of city life, and tours of Fairmount Park would make an excellent itinerary for one day. Philadelphia also needs to distribute a list of perhaps ten one-day tours to the hotels and motels to be given to each guest.

Without a package approach, it is difficult for a tourist to visit Philadelphia. Packaging is important to many businesses. People do not like to have to deal with four or five different businesses in order to accomplish one goal.

7. Shredded Wheat

I saw a campaign by Shredded Wheat that touted the cereal's high nutritional rating by a consumer magazine. But what's Shredded Wheat's problem? Is it that people don't think it's nutritional? Not at all. Shredded Wheat's problem (or advantage, depending on how you look at it) is that it has a unique taste—a taste people either like or dislike. Shredded Wheat would have been better off trying to offer different ways for people to eat its product. It could have incorporated the nutritional information into the commercial, but the emphasis should have been on recipes for enjoying Shredded Wheat. This campaign would address a problem area that is restricting Shredded Wheat's sales.

8. Critical Care Medical Clinic

A sixteen-hour-day, seven-days-a-week medical clinic recently opened in a nearby town. The clinic used a fairly extensive advertising program announcing low prices; however, this program was inappropriate because it did not take into account people's motivation in selecting a professional service.

People do not patronize an M.D. or any service business because of a low price. They go because they have faith in the person dispensing the service. A service business does not have a product someone can inspect by touch or feel. People really don't have a standard to be able to judge a professional, so their evaluation of a service provider is determined by how much trust they have in him or her. Trust is important because the outcome of professional services is unpredictable. For example, a doctor can't cure every patient, a lawyer loses some cases, and an advertising agency does not always achieve the desired market penetration. Unexpected results don't mean, however, that the client did not receive excellent service. If you charge low prices and the clients get less than the desired results, they will probably believe that they received only what they paid for. Next time they'll give their business to someone else.

DIFFICULT MARKETING PROBLEMS

Now that you've read examples of good and bad marketing programs, I'd like you to examine some tough marketing situations and some possible marketing thrusts for these cases.

1. Shoe Store

Your shoe store sells athletic shoes that are, for the most part, premium brands. You have two competitors in your shopping mall—a low-priced store and a premium store. You and the other premium store carry different brands. The other premium store's manufacturer has embarked upon an aggressive national ad campaign with local sports celebrities; it also brings local athletes to the store. Your manufacturer has responded by opening more outlets to keep its market share. What would you do?

Of course, the easy answer is to cut prices, but what if your competitor cuts its prices? What have you gained? The smart move would be to add value to the products you sell. If you are in a mall, much of your exposure occurs as customers walk by. Therefore, you should investigate ways to get those customers to come into the store.

I'd recommend an elaborate in-store display telling how to select the proper sports shoe. Most people are bewildered by the specialization of shoes for each particular sport. A display—and I mean a big display—that the customer could use to select the proper shoe for his or her needs would attract customers. Take advantage of the fact that most stores have poorly trained help. There are two keys to making this strategy work. First, the display must be seen easily from outside the store. Second, the display should be informative and attractive.

Another course of action would be to give out gift certificates offering 10 to 20 percent off at local sports events, fitness spas, and high school activities. While it is a form of price discount, it is not something competition can easily match.

2. Movie Theater

An old movie theater has been reopened by a new owner. The theater shows movies that have already been shown at the major movie houses and charges $1.50. But there are few customers and no response to ads in the paper. One marketing possibility is to go to the local grade schools and give away free tickets—four to each student in one class every week. The lucky class would be selected at random, so the students would never know which class would get the tickets. This tactic could generate enough interest that people would develop a habit of going to this movie house.

3. Large Department Store

You manage a large department store which has been in business for 50 years. Your chain is located primarily in large malls in the suburbs with only one downtown location. The chain was successful moving out to the suburbs in time to catch the suburban boom, but now sales have been eroded as new department stores such as Bloomingdale's have opened with more targeted marketing approaches. Other older department stores in the area have gravitated toward more traditional upscale merchandise. Your chain has continued to provide middle-of-the-road merchandise for the average person, but Sears, K mart, and other discount stores have taken many of your customers. You've countered over the last three or four years with a continuous sales promotion strategy. The promotions worked in the past because of the store's established name, but now people think the store may be setting prices artificially high just to have more promotions. Because of this and the fact that the merchandise is not targeted to any one audience, sales are down significantly, profits are nonexistent, and the store is in grave danger of going out of business. What do you do?

You have a big problem. In fact, most stores in this position close. I think what you have to do is change your selling strategy. Sears did this successfully in my area by completely changing the store layout and calling it the Sears store of the future. The merchandise is displayed on special racks designed just for that product. It's as if merchandise is displayed on a billboard with sales copy on it. It's easy to find merchandise, see what you are buying, and feel confident at the checkout counter.

But what could be done about your store? How about completely changing the merchandise layout to categories of people's seasons as determined by color analysis. Color analysis is currently a big trend. Apparently a person's skin and hair coloring is complemented by colors of one of the four seasons. For instance, my wife is autumn. She looks best in brown, gold, warm reds, orange, yellow, and other warm colors. I can't always remember those colors, but I can remember autumn. Maybe the store could display the colors of various seasons and the skin types which are complemented by them. Or perhaps a free color analysis could be offered.

For men, I think you could offer a similar approach. I've always wanted to be able to enter a store and punch in my height, weight, and hair coloring and have a computer tell me what type of suit would be best for me. Once I was in a store where about 40 styles of clothes were displayed on mannequins which revolved on a lazy-susan conveyor belt. Once I even saw a TV monitor that showed what different clothes look like on you without having to try them on. Maybe in the children's department you could show video tapes of how cute children look in different outfits.

You also could do things like provide a children's playroom; provide a person or department that could help customers select gifts; and hold weekday clinics, for instance, on how to select a wardrobe. Anyone attending the session could get a 20 percent discount on any merchandise within an hour of the class.

Since I am discussing department stores, I'd like to give Sears a little praise, not so much because of their marketing, but because they are always willing to test an idea. I remember when Sears put children's photographers into their stores; it drew families, and Sears kept the photographers. When Sears tried including dental and optometrist services, they didn't work, and Sears dropped them. The point is, Sears is willing to experiment; it is constantly striving to improve its merchandising and services. I think that's smart. Remember, no matter how much preparation you do, how much thought and consideration you give to your marketing programs, you still don't know if a program will work until the campaign is over. So the more experiences you have, the better you will be able to choose your next campaign.

3. Hitachi VCRs

Hitachi is one of 10 to 20 companies making VCRs. Its product is equivalent to other manufacturers'; however, the product doesn't have a single feature to distinguish it in the consumer's mind. Hitachi is not nearly so well known as other brands. It's sold primarily in appliance outlets and lower-cost stores. Hitachi has not penetrated large department stores or other more upscale marketing outlets.

Hitachi has been able to penetrate the low-priced outlets primarily by keeping prices low. Now competitors have matched the low prices, and Hitachi's sales have stopped growing. Outlet salespeople are reluctant to push Hitachi's product over more traditional brands because of Hitachi's poor brand name recognition. Hitachi needs to solidify its position for future growth. It would prefer not to cut prices any further, as low prices are hurting its profitability. What would you do?

One approach is to find a way to differentiate the product. With 10 to 20 competitors, it is not easy to find a unique product feature; therefore, you probably can't differentiate the Hitachi product itself. But you can differentiate the product in some other way. When I did my own little market research on VCRs to find out what people don't like about them, I found one consistent complaint: the instructions are confusing. A friend of mine had a VCR instruction book over 100 pages long! I can sympathize. I have set my VCR only to play tapes because I can't understand the instructions for other operations.

Now think about this for a minute. People are buying a new product; do they want to cope with confusing instructions? No. So here is an area to exploit. It would help distributors too to be able to sell a Hitachi that is easy to operate. Sounds simple, doesn't it? Yet, I think you would be surprised at how many products have one or two features that are irritating to the user.

Another point here is that in a market with as many competitors as the VCR market, you don't usually have to do something outstanding to differentiate your product from that of others and give yourself a little edge. Having the best instruction book won't impact every customer, but it will some. When the store salespeople know they have a customer whose technical expertise stops at plugging in a VCR, they will know which brand to recommend.

4. Technical Test Products

Technical Test Products is a small company manufacturing specialized test equipment. Technical Test Products has two competitors, both about 10 times its size. The company has done well in business by specializing in one small industry. It dominated that field primarily by making special product adaptations to optimize its product performance in that industry. But now the two major competitors have expanded their product lines and switched to a customized systems approach. They also have switched the orientation of their sales personnel from experts in their particular products to experts in end-user applications.

Technical Test Products does not have the financial capability of matching the new products or total systems approaches of the other companies. Nor has it been able to change its salesforce to a systems orientation. Salespeople who are knowledgeable about the industry are not willing to join with a small company where they feel their sales potential may be limited. The salesforce Technical Test Products does have is product oriented and does not understand end-user applications. The specialization Technical Test Products has toward one industry has been negated by the total systems approach of the other companies. What would you do?

Technical Test Products can't match the competition's switch to a systems approach, but it does have superior product knowledge. Its salespeople are better at working the company's product because that's all they know and sell. One of the problems with the equipment for this market is that different types of materials require different test techniques. Each manufacturer has four or five test procedures to account for different materials. Technical Test Products could switch to having 30 procedures. Plus, it could customize its product for any application and promote the customization procedures for different materials. Its specialization would be in the product while its competition's specialization is in systems. In fact, Technical Test Products may have only five procedures which are modified only slightly. But its salespeople can give a superior demonstration; they can make each test procedure look better.

Technical Test Products' policy should be to go on sales calls after the competition has been there. Let the competition explain how its product line fits into a company's operation. Let the competition explain the various components customers need. Then Technical Test Products can come in and show how its product, with superior customization, will give better results. One thing Technical Test Products has going for it is that it is selling to engineers, and engineers usually like to see all possible products before making a decision.

Why may this program work? First, it is within the financial means of the company, a program that Technical Test Products can execute. Second, the program deals with the company's strengths. Any time a competitor becomes strong in one area, it probably has a weak spot somewhere else. Now, in some ways this differentiation is not as significant as it might appear. But the fact is that Technical Test Products' salesforce can set up and instruct a customer on the use of the company's product equipment better than any other company's salesforce. This program should effectively dramatize that benefit.

MARKETING THRUST CHECKLIST

I've covered many ideas for a marketing thrust and how to decide what areas need attacking. I also reviewed quite a few examples to help you think about what marketing strategies or thrusts might work for your business. Now is the time you have to decide on your marketing thrust. But don't just choose one or two. I want you to pick five or six that have possibilities. Force yourself to think of as many as possible. By forcing yourself to list more options, you force yourself to look at more aspects of your business. After you've listed five or six options, follow the checklist I've designed for you. It will help you decide which thrust might work best. I've included six potential marketing thrusts for Hitachi. Each one is evaluated with the checklist. Read the sample section first before doing your own checklist.

As you use the checklist, remember that there are usually negatives to any campaign. Marketing is not like investing; there are no safe, conservative tactics you can use. If you are too conservative, your competitors will outmarket you.

Choose Your Marketing Thrusts

1. _____

2. _____

3. _____

4. _____

5. _____

6. _____

Marketing Thrust Checklist

High _____ Medium _____ Low _____   What impact will this thrust have on your company?

High _____ Medium _____ Low _____   What is the cost of the program?

High _____ Medium _____ Low _____   How risky is the promotion? Can you recover if it doesn't go well?

High _____ Medium _____ Low _____   What is the probability your company can effectively implement the program?

Here is a series of yes and no questions you should ask yourself about each thrust.

Yes_____ No_____   Have you addressed a major problem or opportunity?

Yes_____ No_____   Is your thrust easy to understand?

Yes_____ No_____   Is it meaningful to the customer?

Yes_____ No_____   Does it match the efforts of the rest of your company? For example, don't say you have superb service if manufacturing is cutting inventory.

Yes_____ No_____   Can your organization execute the plan?

Yes_____ No_____   Is your approach consistent with past campaigns? If not, you may want to run an intermediate campaign to prepare your customers. Try to avoid drastic shifts in marketing policy.

Yes_____ No_____   Are you going to be well differentiated from your competitors?

Yes_____ No_____   Are you in conflict with other marketing thrusts in your company? If your company has more than one product with more than one marketing plan, you need to check on what other marketing people are doing.

Yes＿＿ No＿＿ Are you conflicting with any major new programs or products which may be introduced in the near future?

Yes＿＿ No＿＿ Will this program allow you to meet your sales volume goals?

Yes＿＿ No＿＿ Will this program be within your expense limitations?

Yes＿＿ No＿＿ Will this program allow you to meet your price objectives?

Yes＿＿ No＿＿ Will this program match your market's expectations for promotional activity?

Yes＿＿ No＿＿ Does this program influence the pertinent people in the buying decision?

Yes＿＿ No＿＿ Are the results you expect consistent with results that have been achieved in the past, either by your or your competitors?

Yes＿＿ No＿＿ Will your price be in line with the price/value/feature relationship the market expects?

Yes＿＿ No＿＿ Are there any major problems, opportunities, or events coming up soon that this program may hurt?

Yes＿＿ No＿＿ Does this program have a beneficial long-term impact?

Yes＿＿ No＿＿ Will the program have a detrimental long-term impact?

Yes＿＿ No＿＿ Does the program improve your product's defensibility?

Yes＿＿ No＿＿ Will the program work well for your salesforce? Will your salesforce like it?

HITACHI'S USE OF THE CHECKLIST

Hitachi's marketing people have decided that they have four major problems:

1. Poor brand recognition.
2. Poor distributor support.
3. Poor product differentiation.
4. Lower-than-industry-average pricing and profits.

Hitachi's sales are $221 million, and its total promotional budget is $9.6 million. The promotion money includes the value of discounts in excess of 10 percent. (Hitachi's budget allows 10 percent discounts to dealers through quantity purchases and seasonal programs.) Hitachi has decided to consider six possible marketing thrusts.

1. Operate a nationwide advertising campaign stressing Hitachi's position as one of the world's top technological companies. (Hitachi is actually one of the top semiconductor and computer companies in the world. It is a strong high-tech company, but it is weak in consumer goods.)

2. Target a features/benefits program at sports and movie buffs— two of the largest VCR segments. Either a cable TV or a magazine campaign could be directed at them.

3. Introduce a new, easier-to-use instruction manual which would be four-color and include numerous illustrations. The company would design a slide rule chart outlining each step for each VCR procedure. The program would be directed to the consumer through targeted media advertising. Store display materials would also be provided. The new manual and store displays would cost $3 million, leaving $6.6 million for media advertising.

4. Run an aggressive program to retail outlets offering sales incentives, extended terms, and large discounts. The outlets and salesforce have said that aggressive discounts would substantially increase sales.

5. Introduce a new, easy-to-use instruction manual. This would be less elaborate than the one of program 3, but still an improvement over anything in the market. Also included would be a retail outlet introduction program, dealer displays, and a media program. This program differs from 3 because it has a $1 million introduction to the outlets. Also, the instruction manual is not so adventuresome as 3, leaving money for a dealer introduction program.

6. Introduce an easy-to-use manual similar to thrust 5, and coordinate it with a major dealer program. The big difference is that a large dealer introduction program would be included, along with co-op advertising rather than 5's media campaign.

In the following analysis, Hitachi will have the same $9.6 million marketing expense budget for each program. For each thrust, the points that are particularly important are circled. A discussion at the end of the ratings chart will explain the pluses and minuses of each thrust. A point to remember when reading the analysis is that all of these thrusts appear to be reasonable, and a given company might choose any of the six; however, the checklist will help you determine the best thrust.

	1	2	3	4	5	6
What impact will this thrust have on your company?	High	Med	Med	Med	Med	Med
What is the cost of the program?	High	Med	Med	Med	Med	Med
How risky is the promotion?	(High)	Low	Low	(High)	Med	Med
How probable is it that the program will be properly implemented?	(Low)	Med	Med	Med	Med	Med
Have you addressed a major problem or opportunity?	Yes	Yes	Yes	Yes	Yes	Yes
Is your thrust easy to understand?	Yes	Yes	Yes	Yes	Yes	(Yes)
Is it meaningful?	Yes	Yes	Yes	(?)	Yes	Yes
Does it match the efforts of the rest of your company?	Yes	Yes	Yes	Yes	Yes	Yes
Can your organization execute the plan?	Yes	Yes	(?)	Yes	Yes	Yes
Is the approach consistent with past campaigns?	No	(No)	(No)	Yes	Yes	(Yes)
Are you differentiated?	No	No	Yes	No	Yes	Yes
Are you in conflict with other company programs?	No	No	No	No	No	No
Are you conflicting with anticipated new programs?	No	No	No	No	No	No
Will you meet your sales goals?	?	Yes	(?)	Yes	(?)	Yes
Can you afford this program?	(?)	Yes	Yes	?	Yes	Yes
Will you meet your price objectives?	Yes	Yes	Yes	No	Yes	Yes
Will the program match the market's expectations for promotional activity?	?	(?)	No	Yes	Yes	(Yes)
Does the program influence all the key people in the buying decision?	No	No	Yes	No	Yes	Yes
Are the results you expect consistent with past programs?	Yes	Yes	(?)	(No)	Yes	Yes
Will your price/value relationship be acceptable?	Yes	Yes	Yes	Yes	Yes	Yes
Is there anything happening in the market that could hurt you?	No	No	No	No	No	No
Does the program have a beneficial long-term impact?	Yes	Yes	Yes	No	Yes	Yes
Will the program have a detrimental long-term impact?	No	No	No	(?)	No	No
Does the program improve your product's defensibility?	Yes	Yes	Yes	No	Yes	Yes
Will the program work for your salesforce? Will it like the program?	No	No	?	Yes	(?)	Yes

Program 1

A national advertising program could enhance Hitachi's image and have a positive impact on sales; however a 30-second national TV spot costs $100,000 to $300,000. It's also necessary to run an ad a minimum of five to seven times per week to be effective. This is a high-risk program because Hitachi may not be able to afford to advertise enough to enhance its image. For this reason, I doubt that this program could be successfully implemented.

Hitachi has always directed its programs toward retail outlets, making this program inconsistent with past promotions. It won't help to differentiate the product, as it is primarily an image program. The next key question is, what type of promotion activity do Hitachi's retail outlets expect? It's not clear how they would respond to a national advertising program. In the past, not only Hitachi, but most other VCR manufacturers, have run programs focused on their outlets. This will also impact the salesforce, which spends 90 percent of its time calling on outlets. The salesforce is unlikely to appreciate this program shift.

Overall, raising consumer awareness could increase the company's long-term defensibility and sales volume, but it will be difficult to execute it properly within Hitachi's budget. Also, it's switching Hitachi's emphasis from outlets to consumers. This can be risky when it's uncertain what benefits will result.

Program 2

The emphasis here is on choosing a smaller target market for a concentrated marketing effort. While Hitachi would give up the possibility of impacting the total market, it could be fairly certain it will make a penetration of this segment. Since Hitachi's market share is low, this strategy could improve sales, as well as strenghten its long-term market position.

The problem with the program is that it shifts from its past push strategy to that of a pull program. This is especially dangerous because of the influence of salespeople at the retail level. A customer walks into a retail store and sees five to seven brands of VCRs. Which one he buys will depend, most likely, on the retail salesperson.

This program would be effective if Hitachi had enough brand recognition that consumers would insist on its product. For example, Serta has a very strong name in bedding. If a customer walks into a store and asks for Serta, the salesperson will sell it to him or her. Hitachi doesn't have that power, and without it, this program's switch in direction probably won't produce the desired results.

Program 3

Hitachi's plan here is to totally overhaul its instruction manual, going to four colors, using numerous illustrations, and incorporating other aids such as slide rule charts, and then promote the program through targeted media advertising. The first question about this program is: Can it be implemented? This is a tall order. Hitachi could spend much of its budget only to discover that while its manual is an improvement, it's not that much better.

This program does have several advantages. It's a combination push and pull program. Retail salespeople will probably be able to use the manual as a good closing tool for reluctant buyers, and consumers will appreciate its clarity. If the retail salespeople receive the program enthusiastically, it could produce outstanding benefits. Store display materials and a limited media program will enhance the possibility of the consumer noticing Hitachi's new instruction materials.

The drawback is that since retail salespeople sell many products and lines, it is difficult to focus their attention on one. No other manufacturer has ever run a program quite like this, so it's difficult to gauge how well it will do. I believe this program puts too much emphasis on one item. It's also changing most of the program's emphasis to the customer. The final manual might not be sufficient to make up for the momentum lost in reducing outlet promotions.

Program 4

This program goes back to an all-out attempt to influence distribution outlets. (In VCR distribution, *dealers* and *retail outlets* refer to locations where the consumer buys the product.) Hitachi has always run programs directed to its outlets. The last one was ineffective. Its outlets told the salesforce that bigger discounts were needed and the salesforce would like to fulfill this need.

This is a high-risk program. The last program didn't work; there was not enough incentive to be meaningful. Hitachi can't be sure what level of discounts will be effective. The salesforce wants to offer a 25 percent discount, which is 15 percent over the standard 10 percent. But sales will have to increase 30 percent to break even. It will be difficult to generate a 30 percent sales increase.

Long term, the program could be disastrous because it gives up control to the outlets. Hitachi isn't getting any pull through contact with the consumer. And it's possible that outlets will continue to demand larger discounts. This could cut into profits to the extent that Hitachi will be unable to ever mount a consumer program. This could eventually force it out of the market.

One last comment here is that an outlet's prime interest is in making a sale. To do that it needs an advantage over the competition. If every outlet gets the same low price, no outlet really has an edge; one outlet is no better off than before the discount. When an outlet wants a low price, it wants a price lower than its competitors'.

Program 5

In program 3, Hitachi puts total effort into developing a good instructional manual. This "go for broke" strategy introduces a risk that the manual might not live up to expectations. Program 5 scales back the instruction manual effort, and instead spends $1 million to introduce the program to outlets. Included will be a sales incentive contest offering cash bonuses and a cruise. A special flyer explaining how Hitachi uses the new instruction manual as a sales tool would also be included.

To help emphasize the program, a targeted media campaign similar to program 3's would be initiated.

I believe this program is better than 3 because it's easier to execute and involves less risk. Here the program works with outlet salespeople to teach them to promote the new installation and instruction manual. Program 3 relies on the salespeople understanding the program on their own. Again, the two reasons to be cautious are the uncertainty of the new instructions' effectiveness and the difficulty in impacting outlet salespeople.

This is a strong program. It hits all the key people in the buying decision, positions the product favorably, and helps Hitachi's long-term image in the market. The only danger is that the program switches a considerable percentage of the promotional emphasis from the outlet to the consumer. If necessary, that is a risk Hitachi should be willing to take. The program offers a mix of outlet versus consumer activity. It should keep the outlets somewhat satisfied and at the same time attract the consumer loyalty that is needed for long-term success.

Program 6

This is the program I would select. It is similar to program 5 except that it has a much larger dealer introduction program, spending $2 million versus $1 million, and impacts the consumer through co-op advertising rather than through a typical media campaign.

The reason I prefer this program is that it is closer to Hitachi's traditional programs. It still concentrates on the outlet while at the same time uses co-op advertising to direct a message to the consumer. Hitachi needs to project its image to the market, and this program accomplishes that while still promoting to retail outlets. Next year I would direct more promotional programs toward the consumer.

Chapter 8

GETTING YOUR CUSTOMERS TO NOTICE

Within the past two years, wine coolers have been introduced in the United States with great success. Friends of mine who drink wine coolers tell me they taste like a mix of wine and a lemon-lime soft drink, such as 7UP. The creation of wine coolers is not a technological breakthrough like compact discs, nor are wine coolers receiving favorable reviews like the Ford Taurus. What wine coolers have is a great marketing program.

Bartles & Jaymes's campaign to introduce wine coolers met all six steps of an effective marketing implementation program.

1. *Know your target market.* Wine coolers are light, refreshing drinks for people who don't like beer. Every step of Bartles & Jaymes's implementation plan shows that the company identified its target market.

2. *Create an effective message.* The term *wine cooler* is sensational. *Wine* implies a light, alcoholic drink, and *cooler* implies a refreshing drink. The name suggests that wine coolers are a substitute for beer, gin and tonics, or soft drinks.

3. *Enhance the message with your promotional strategy.* Wine coolers are a light drink for casual social affairs. Bartles and Jaymes's commercials with the two older men in overalls are light, funny, and right in the spirit of wine coolers.

4. *Choose the right communications strategy.* Wine coolers are a nonessential, frequent purchase, calling for a strategy that makes the customer aware of the product. Bartles & Jaymes's commercials are widely displayed and memorable.

5. *Maximize the effectiveness of the distribution channel.* The first time I saw Bartles & Jaymes wine coolers, they were the focal point in a large display next to the entrance to a store.

6. *Reinforce your message with every customer contact.* I like wine coolers' packaging. Its bottle is like a beer bottle, and wine coolers are sold in four-packs, resembling a six-pack of beer. I was impressed with the thoroughness of Bartles & Jaymes's campaign to communicate that wine coolers are substitutes for beer.

Chapters 1–6 are a checklist of business areas to consider as possible targets for a marketing strategy. Chapter 7 discusses how to create an effective strategy. This chapter explains tactics you might use to implement that strategy. It's divided into six sections:

1. Creating an effective message.
2. Enhancing the message.
3. Choosing a communication strategy.
4. Communication tactics.
5. Maximizing the efforts of your distribution channel.
6. Thinking big when introducing a new program.

As you read this chapter, write down every tactic you might use to communicate your marketing program. Be sure that each tactic in the program supports the product's image. Too often marketers develop excellent strategies but neglect to attend to every last detail. Those last details can determine if a program will succeed or fail.

CREATING AN EFFECTIVE MESSAGE

Marketing Slogans

Businesses should have a phrase that is easy to remember and that captures the essense of their marketing focus. If your campaign is building from past successes, you probably already have a good slogan. Make certain to keep placing that slogan before the public. When I think of Ford, I think of "Quality is job one." That's all I think about Ford unless I'm buying a car or analyzing Ford's marketing campaigns. People remember very little about a company. Remember, as important as a program is to you, it is not that important to the public. Therefore, a slogan often becomes the only thing a customer remembers about your product. Even though a potential customer may not need your product now, he or she may remember your slogan and be influenced by it when making a future purchase.

There are three points to consider about slogans. First, make sure the slogan has an important or meaningful message. "Quality is job one" is an important message. "Campbell's soup is good food" is a direct, effective slogan. "Heartbeat of America" is not a significant message. Chrysler's "The pride is back" is more meaningful because Chrysler is proud of the cars it makes. Burger King's "Have it your way" is an excellent slogan because it tells why Burger King is different. "Spend a night, not a fortune" is another slogan that conveys a meaningful point.

Second, make sure your slogan is easy to remember. Good slogans are short and catchy. In fact, you might even incorporate your name in the slogan. Nestlé's slogan is really just "Nestlé's chocolate"—hard to forget. Pepsi's "Taste of a new generation" and Tandy's "Nothing beats a Tandy" are also short, catchy slogans.

Third, make sure your slogan reinforces your marketing thrust. Charles Schwab's slogan of "America's largest discount brokerage" relates well to its campaigns. Both Advil's "Advanced medicine for pain" and Mercedez-Benz's "Engineered like no other car in the world" effectively reinforce marketing thrusts.

In some cases, successful companies don't have recognizable slogans. McDonald's doesn't have one, but it does have the visual images of Ronald McDonald and the golden arches. Kellogg's doesn't have a slogan either, but each of its products has a recognizable image, such as Tony the Tiger. Pillsbury uses the dough boy. Symbolic figures or representations are excellent alternatives to slogans.

The Name

The name of your product or service is important. Ideally it should identify the purpose of the product or service. Jiffy Lube, 7-Eleven, Thriftway, and Dollar Rent-A-Car are examples of ideal names. You might consider changing your company's name to reflect what you are doing, especially when there has been a major change in your focus or a merger. For instance, when Sperry and Burroughs merged, they changed their names to one—Unisys. They did so because they wanted it clear that Unisys was a new force in the marketplace.

When Esso changed its name to Exxon, it was identifying itself as an updated, modern company. Datsun publicizing itself as Nissan is another example. Until the name change, Datsun sold either inexpensive small sedans or sports cars. Once it decided to sell a wider range of cars, Datsun changed its name to Nissan.

A name change creates many options for new promotions and even celebrations; it helps create excitement. Of course, if your name is known and respected, keep it. But if your name is not an asset, don't be afraid to change it.

Store Sign or Company Logo

I can't emphasize enough the importance of your building's or store's appearance. The sign should be attractive and describe your business. The logo should be your trademark. The logo of a restaurant by my house spells out its name, Pastabilities, with spaghetti noodles. The logo makes it clear that the restaurant serves Italian food.

Businesses that are not stores can publicize their names and logos at conventions; on statements, letters, advertisements, and literature; and in a variety of other locations. Never pass up an appropriate opportunity to exhibit your name and logo.

Your sign should indicate more than the name of the store or business; it should imply your purpose and target market. If your store is one for upscale consumers, your sign should imply that. If you cater to an economy market, make sure the sign conveys that impression. For example, K mart's signs do an effective job of conveying an economy store image.

ENHANCING THE MESSAGE

Pricing Strategy

Pricing strategy not only changes the marketing message, it also helps attract target customers. For example, when Ford introduced the Taurus, it had several pricing options. Ford could have priced the Taurus at $12,000, targeting the American family car market. Or Ford could have priced the Taurus at $19,000, targeting the upscale sedan market and competing with Audis and BMWs. If the Taurus were priced between $12,000 and $19,000, it would be in a dangerous marketing position, priced too high for the American sedan market and not priced high enough to compete with the upscale foreign cars. Ford chose to price the Taurus at $12,000 so that it was targeted at the American family sedan buyer.

You must be careful about setting price because once a price has been set, it establishes the product's worth. For example, if Ford raised the price of the Taurus to $20,000, its sales would fall dramatically. Consumers have already established that the Taurus is worth $12,000.

Earlier you read that there is an emotional reaction involved with most purchases. This reaction is influenced by the image of the product, and the image is influenced by price. Imagine these two sales pitches. "Yes, my price is the highest. But that's because it's the best. We have the product for the people who want the best." And, "Why is our price less? We are trying to give you a better value. Our product has all the features of the higher-priced ones." If you are image conscious, which product would you buy? Surprisingly enough, the company with the lower-priced product may need to spend more on advertising and promotion to establish an image than the company with the premium product.

Make certain that your pricing strategy fits your marketing campaign. Do you want to tout your car as the fastest on the road and then have a low price? If you have the fastest car, charge for it. It will make your image more believable. If your price is too low, you may need a strategy to move the price up in stages. For example, Renault set a low price on the Alliance and then stressed the dependability of the Alliance in an advertising campaign featuring George C. Scott. Instead of stressing dependability and low price, Renault should have said that it had added features to make the care more dependable, that a more dependable car was not available in this price range. And then I would have increased the price. After all, Renault would have touted the changes and improvements that make the car more dependable. What good are those changes if Renault wasn't willing to charge for them? The public knows no business can survive without a profit.

Promotion Strategy

If it's appropriate, you could use a nonadvertising promotion to help initiate a new marketing program. For instance, you could introduce a car with an extra feature such as leather upholstery for only an additional $500 on the first 10,000 cars sold. Customers know that leather upholstery would normally add $2,000 to the car's price, so you have not compromised your actual product price, even though you have offered a favorable discount.

Another program could offer a promotional package to distributors which included promotional signs for their windows, ad slicks for the local media, and a 20 percent discount when they buy an equivalent of three months' worth of inventory. Explain to the distributor that the discount is a bonus for its ad campaign promoting your product. This type of program promotes favorable product exposure to the final consumer without compromising your image.

If you have a retail store, concentrate on having clowns, sports celebrities, or other interesting in-house attractions to promote a change in marketing direction.

I want to stress that you should be cautious about making drastic changes in your usual promotional strategy; customers get used to a company's strategy and don't like sudden changes. If you have always had big sales promotions, don't stop having them. You need a program to gradually phase out sales promotions. If they are necessary, try to restructure them to offer nonprice discounts so they don't compromise the product's image.

Another pitfall is having too many promotions. As in all marketing, consistency counts. It takes time to implement a promotion. A promotion's effectiveness will be increased by keeping the program simple and consistent with past campaigns. Customers need to understand a promotion, or it won't be effective. For example, the Roy Rogers restaurants had a promotion that I almost figured out before the program ended. The program wasn't simple or long enough to have an effect on me.

Market Research

You may coordinate a market research program with the marketing plan. For instance, a marketing thrust may be that a home-improvement store cares about the neighborhood. If research found that most of the residents like early American decor, then the store could adjust its merchandise to favor the early American look.

Another example is Pepsi. Pepsi decided to reinforce its campaign that it was better tasting than Coke. To help prove its point, Pepsi conducted market research on how the consumer rated the taste of Pepsi compared to the taste of Coke.

Or an industrial company may find that its current market is too small. The company may not know how to penetrate other markets or what markets are most appropriate to expand into. The company might direct a market research campaign to product development engineers, hoping to find new applications for its product.

Market research should be used whenever you want to make a change, but aren't sure how you want to change. For instance, you want your company to be the top testing company in a particular industry, but you don't know how to accomplish this. You are not knowledgeable about your own strengths, the market's demands, or industry needs that are not being met. You might want to delay introducing any major program until your market research indicates which strategies you should use.

Segmenting and Targeting Your Market

Your strategy or thrust may work better in one market segment than in another. If so, define the market segment you are targeting, and orient your program toward it. For example, when my father added a senior citizen consignment handcraft boutique to his store, he stopped advertising in the paper and sent direct mail to senior citizens.

I mentioned earlier that Ford used pricing tactics to target the American family sedan market. I think Ford may have wanted to introduce the Taurus to eventually compete with the upscale foreign sedans. But Ford felt that European sedan customers didn't believe a Ford fit their image of an upscale car.

Positioning Statement

Every company should have for each product a positioning statement that explains the company's business strategy. For example, Burger King's positioning statement would be something like this:

> Burger King is a fast food restaurant alternative to McDonald's. Burger King will sell food similar to, yet slightly different from, McDonald's. If at all possible, Burger King's outlets will be placed close to McDonald's.

This has been a successful positioning statement for Burger King. Customers like a change of pace when eating at fast-food restaurants. Burger King's campaign of "Have it your way" clearly fits this positioning statement.

Examine how your marketing strategy or thrust fits your company's positioning statement. If your strategy doesn't fit, you should either change your thrust or change your positioning statement. It is essential that your marketing thrust support your positioning statement.

Consider, for example, the Record Revolution in my neighborhood. The Record Revolution is a record store whose marketing thrust is having low prices. Record Revolution's positioning statement is that it is a small, convenient record store in the neighborhood. It could offer coupons at high school dances for $2 off any record; place discount coupons in the high school newspaper; or offer a discount to anyone who brings in a ticket stub from a local high school football game.

CHOOSING A COMMUNICATION STRATEGY

What type of communication should you use? The answer depends on whether the purchase category of your product is:

- Infrequent, but necessary.
- Infrequent and unnecessary.
- Frequent.
- Based on trust.
- Not many potential customers.

Customers approach each type of purchase differently, so it is essential that your marketing program match communications with the customer's purchase process. This section outlines the different types of purchases and the correct type of communication strategy for each.

Infrequent, Necessary Purchases

Recently I wanted to buy a specialized plastic container for a printed circuit board assembly station. This was the first and maybe only time I would purchase this product. I looked for suppliers by searching through the press releases and ads in industrial magazines. I found five potential suppliers, requested literature about their products, and chose the one I thought met my needs. There may have been other suppliers, but I didn't have time to search for them.

If your product is necessary but purchased infrequently, customers need to be able to find it. Yellow Pages ads, product directories, and conventions are some ways to inform customers of your product and where to buy it.

People don't often buy carpets and appliances, but when they do, they feel they are necessary purchases. There is a strip mall near my home which has both a carpet and an appliance store. When I needed to buy a carpet, I bought it at the carpet store, but when I needed a kitchen appliance, I shopped elsewhere.

Why? The carpet store's sign was large and descriptive; there were attractive displays in the windows; and since none of the area carpet stores do much advertising, the store in the strip mall was the one I remembered most. On the other hand, some appliance stores in my area advertise heavily and these were the ones I remembered.

If your product is one that is purchased infrequently, be aware of what the competition is doing, and make certain that your prospective customers are adequately exposed to your product.

Infrequent, Unnecessary Purchases

There is a specialty shopping village 45 miles from my home. Recently my wife went there and purchased two flower vases. She went to the village because it was having a strawberry festival. Although she had always wanted to go to this shopping village, she needed an extra incentive to actually do so.

People just don't run out to buy things they don't need. It takes effort to entice customers to come to you when a purchase is unnecessary, and a program with high-impact advertising is called for. The shopping village would probably be wasting its money if it ran a 52-week promotion program. It is more profitable for the village to stage occasional dramatic promotions. After an initial visit, customers are more likely to return. But to entice the customer to make the first visit requires a program with pizzazz.

Marketers often don't realize most purchases by a company are infrequent and unnecessary. Consider a company which sells nuts and bolts. Its prospective customers may buy nuts and bolts all the time, but only occasionally will a buyer choose a new supplier. A buying decision is made only when a buyer considers a new supplier.

Why is the decision unnecessary? After all, the customer must buy nuts and bolts. The reason the purchase is unnecessary is that the buyer does not have to consider switching suppliers. He or she could continue to buy from the current vendor.

I think many suppliers to other businesses should run one or two dramatic programs a year. It might compel prospective customers to consider switching vendors.

Frequent Purchases

My wife buys groceries at any one of three nearby supermarkets. How does she decide which of the three to shop at? After she reads the sales circulars which come each week, she shops at the store that has her favorite meat products on sale. A supermarket must constantly send its message to its target customer.

Coke, Pepsi, Budweiser, and Miller all sell products that are frequent purchases. They too are constantly advertising to keep their names before the public. If your product is purchased frequently, be sure customers are constantly exposed to your name.

Based on Trust

Trust is the backbone of many service businesses as well as virtually all professional practices. The best way to generate trust is person-to-person contact. Politicians have known this for years. Every time a politician campaigns, he or she can be found meeting people face to face.

I sometimes sense that marketers forget the value of a face-to-face meeting—after all, direct marketing, telemarketing, and ad programs work toward minimizing face-to-face contact. A marketing manager once told me that he thought a young lawyer's marketing program was unsophisticated, because he had joined a country club, the Chamber of Commerce, and the Jaycees. I don't think the lawyer's program was unsophisticated. After all, face-to-face contact is an excellent marketing tool for his product.

Another factor that builds trust is visibility. The more your product is visible to customers, the more they will trust you. For example, if you're a contractor doing four out of five remodeling jobs in my neighborhood, I'll probably trust you. A lawyer or doctor who is visible in a community generates the same type of trust.

Not Many Customers

Some industrial products are sold to a small but scattered market. These products usually can't support a large advertising budget. To be successful, a company must identify its prospects. Once they have been identified, the industrial company can either make a personal sales call or institute a direct marketing campaign.

Obtaining the names of prospects requires a slightly different strategy than that of most marketing communications. Usually a communications strategy tries to create customer interest in the product. To get names requires you only to get someone interested enough to send for more information. A realtor recently sent me a postcard offering instructions on how to make an extra $3,000 when selling a house. That was an effective tool for finding potential home sellers.

Once I was responsible for marketing industrial test equipment which had a small, scattered market. The most effective tool I developed for getting names was a short, three-paragraph letter simply explaining that the equipment was a thickness measurement device, listing the equipment's five ideal applications, and asking if the recipient would like to receive two published articles. The letter covered a third of a page. I experienced a sharp drop in response rate every time I added an extra paragraph to the letter.

Other tactics which work well for reaching a small, scattered target are card packs, press releases, and conventions.

COMMUNICATION TACTICS

Ad Strategy

Americans are bombarded with ad messages every day, and no one can remember more than a small percentage of the ads that he or she is exposed to. That is why it is important for your ad to be effective. The first key tactic of any effective campaign is running an ad repeatedly. Don't pin your campaign around one big ad; you are better off choosing one segment of the market and then advertising to it often, rather than trying to reach a general market with less frequent ads.

A second key advertising tactic is to grab the prospects' attention fast—very fast. People will usually give an ad only one or two seconds. If an ad doesn't pass this hurdle, it won't be effective.

A third key tactic is to get your message across in five to eight seconds. An ad may grab attention, but not hold it for a reading of the entire ad. So if you want exposure to be effective, get your message across quickly.

A final guideline is not to use a lot of copy. My experience is that a customer is turned off by too much copy.

I can't emphasize enough that you restrain yourself in running an ad campaign. There are probably many people who can buy your product, and you might want to reach them all—don't. Restrict yourself to only those who can be reached effectively. There is nothing wrong with running ads in local newspapers or scheduling an ad on a cable channel rather than on a regular commercial channel.

Advertising is a complex field. Following are a few paragraphs explaining various advertising methods; however, I can't do advertising justice in this book. If you want more information, get a book on advertising. Just remember, a marketer is looking at ads to see if they are delivering the proper message to the appropriate customer. Look to see if an ad's emphasis is pertinent and easy to understand, and if the ad has the proper strength for your goals.

1. Television is a useful tactic for reaching a large audience with an effective visual message. TV's two drawbacks are that it's difficult to target an audience, and it's expensive.

TV ads are useful if you can afford a steady year-round ad campaign to raise customer awareness or you have a dramatic short-term event that requires customer action. For example, a TV ad program would be an effective promotion for a tent sale sponsored by five car dealers.

2. Radio ads have the advantage of being less expensive than TV ads. Radio is also a better medium for targeting your customers. But a message on radio lacks TV's visual image and is not an effective medium for introducing a new message.

Radio ads work well in conjunction with a TV ad campaign. They help support the message and remind the listener of the TV ad. Radio ads are also effective if the product is known. Windsor Shirts is an established chain of stores in the Philadelphia area, allowing it to effectively use radio advertising to promote its sales.

3. Newspapers, like TV and radio, are excellent media for generating immediate customer action. If you are going to have a big sale, a newspaper is a good place to advertise.

Newspapers also play a role that's often overlooked. People who are "red hot" prospects for an infrequent purchase often look first at newspaper ads to see who is having a sale. You will lose sales if your competitors are advertising in the newspapers and you are not. Consider using newspaper ads if your product is an infrequent purchase, such as carpeting or appliances.

Newspaper ads have a big advantage over radio and TV ads because they provide the reader with a reference source. TV and radio ads are over in 30 seconds. The newspaper is still in the prospect's possession long after he or she has noticed an ad.

While newspapers are excellent for quick action, they don't work well for image or features/benefits ads.

4. Yellow pages and product directories are tools customers utilize when they are looking for a product or service. Typically customers looking at yellow pages are excellent sales prospects.

Before putting a big ad in the yellow pages or a product directory, remember that often customers don't look at ads if they already know where to buy the product. For example, a couple may want to buy a new mattress. They won't use the yellow pages if they've already seen five ads in the paper. If your major competitors are advertising on TV or the radio, it's questionable if customers will see your ad in the yellow pages.

People who open the yellow pages are naturally attracted to the big ads; therefore, businesses with large ads will attract a higher number of customers. Don't have a smaller ad than your competitor.

One last point about yellow page advertising—people typically go to the businesses that are closest to their homes. Try to give your ad enough appeal to entice customers to travel the extra distance to your store or business. Make your ad different from your competitors', and let it suggest that your store is worth a little extra travel time.

You should use yellow page advertising if you have a product or service which is usually found only by using the phone book.

5. Magazine ads are the best tactic for targeting an audience. For example, advertisements in *Vogue* are directed at women interested in fashion.

A magazine's ability to target a market is especially true in business-to-business marketing where every industry has a minimum of three to four specialized magazines. Another advantage of magazine ads is that they are effective for a long time. Customers might refer back to your ad for over a year as a reference source.

The disadvantage of magazine ads is that they may reach only a small number of potential prospects. Many prospects might not read a magazine, and others may read a magazine but not the ads. This lack of readership is offset, at least in part, by the fact that a magazine ad can have a strong impact when read.

Some industry magazines are actually guides to new products. The editorial content consists of new product releases. Often businesses save new products magazines to use as a reference. Advertise in a new products magazine if your industry has one.

6. Card packs are becoming a popular advertising medium. A card pack contains postcards from 35 to 100 different companies which are targeted at an identifiable customer, such as a new business owner.

A postcard mailer placed in a card pack needs to be short and dramatic. It also needs to inspire a customer to buy a product or to request more information. The advantages of card packs are that they effectively target a market, and they are cost effective. The disadvantage is that a card pack may reach only a small segment of the target customers. Like magazines, many people don't look at card packs, and others only look through a few of the postcards.

Card packs can supplement an ad campaign. They can't deliver your message to most of your target market, but they can add incremental exposure.

Public Relations

Public relations, or PR, is one of the most effective ways of communicating your message. Editors, especially those with smaller publications, love interesting stories; they have trouble filling their newspapers or magazines with articles. PR can be as valuable for a small retail business as it is for a major corporation.

There are two types of public relations you should consider: short one- or two-paragraph fill-ins, and major stories. A short release with "FOR IMMEDIATE RELEASE" at the top of the page can be sent to local newspapers with an announcement about your business. Always include a picture if you can. I recommend that you send out releases whenever you make significant changes in your business. Only 5 to 10 percent may be published, but they are effective when printed.

For a major story, you need to first arrange a meeting with a local newspaper or magazine editor. Share an interesting fact about your business, such as how you started, what made you decide to go into business, unusual products you offer, or the unique layout of your store. Tell the editor about your ideas for a story and ask him or her if the story might be of interest. Ever wonder how a story gets into the paper about someone starting a business? Just like this. If your marketing thrust is about to change, I think you should try to get an article about it published in the local paper or industry journal.

Another way of using PR is to sponsor events or give away door prizes at local fundraisers. McDonald's sponsors golf classics, all-star high school basketball games, and Ronald McDonald houses.

Direct Mail

Direct mail can be an effective tool for any marketing campaign. You can do several things with direct mail: first, you can familiarize prospects with your firm; second, you may make an immediate sale; and third, you may entice a reader to contact your company for more information.

Again, with direct mail, like all advertising, it's repetition that makes it effective. Just one mailing may get you some customers, but five or six mailings to the same customers will help them remember you when they eventually need your product or service.

I always like to support a program with direct mail. For instance, if a retail outlet installs a new display of your products, why not pump direct mail into his area to tout the products? Also mention the store's new display in the mailing; the retailer will be impressed and delighted with your strong support.

If you are considering using direct mail to sell your product, I recommend that you research the topic thoroughly. Again, it is beyond the scope of this book to go into everything involved in generating an effective direct mail promotion.

Before I go on, I'd like to comment on repetition. When I use the term, I don't necessarily mean running your ad every other month. Multiple exposure is the key. If I'm on a restricted budget, I prefer an intense one- or two-month campaign to a longer but less repetitive campaign. By repeating a message over and over during a short period, I'll successfully communicate it. For instance, for a time it seemed like Alka Seltzer was the most frequent advertiser on TV. But when Alka Seltzer's market position was established, it sharply reduced its advertising.

Companies often conduct intense programs in traditionally slow seasons. That means they are sending their message when the fewest number of people are in the market. Doesn't it make more sense to run a program when the most people are in the market?—then it will produce more sales. I like running programs when demand is highest unless the company is unable to meet the increased demand.

Conventions

Conventions offer an opportunity to effectively display your product and to get new customers. At a convention, your company may appear larger than it really is, enhancing the company image. I recommend that you get a copy of your local business paper and watch for pertinent conventions in your area. Then visit the conventions to see if any might be appropriate for your products. Conventions, especially the smaller ones, can be profitable if you have a specialty product or store. Conventions are a place where potential customers, who otherwise might be difficult to locate, can learn about your business.

If you are a manufacturer, watch your industry trade magazines for conventions which may be of interest to you. Conventions are useful for exposing a product to a large number of potential prospects for a fairly low cost. Also my experience has been that customers with an immediate need like to go to conventions to see what is available to meet that need. Your sales volume may suffer if you don't take advantage of conventions.

Plant and Manufacturing Tours

If it's appropriate to your message, consider conducting plant tours. Ford could have used plant tours to emphasize the slogan "Quality is job one." Ford has plants across the United States; to have opened these plants for planned tours would have been a great marketing tool to show firsthand that Ford makes quality cars.

One company I worked for gave factory tours. To those of us

who worked there, our factory looked dull, messy, and unimpressive, but our customers thought the factory operation was fascinating. Why? Previously they had no idea what was involved in making our product. They couldn't believe how many manufacturing steps were necessary, nor the height of our quality control.

Factory tours project a strong message: We are very proud of what we do. Consider having your next distributor or sales meeting at your plant.

Telemarketing

Telemarketing, or telephone marketing, can be used as either a follow-up technique or for cold call canvassing. It works well following up with a prospect who has requested information or taken some other action to indicate interest in your product. It can verify that a person is a prospect and can also overcome obstacles that might prevent a customer from making a purchase.

I've never liked telemarketing as a cold calling technique. I believe it's rude to phone someone who has not expressed an interest in your product. Nevertheless, telemarketing with cold calls can work.

Telemarketing is capable of accomplishing two tasks at once. First, it generates customer interest with an opening teaser; then the caller immediatedly tries to close the sale. Telemarketing is more effective than direct mail because it doesn't give the prospect a chance to "cool off." A customer can more easily set aside a letter than cut off a phone call.

The big problem today with telemarketing is that it is overused and may be losing its effectiveness. Last week 11 telemarketing people called me or my wife. I have neither the time nor the inclination to listen to that many sales pitches.

Canvassing

Canvassing is often thought of as door-to-door selling, either to commercial prospects or to people in a neighborhood. Canvassing is one of the marketing techniques that build customer trust. A home remodeling contractor, for example, requires customer trust, and as a rule, people don't trust someone they've never met. Therefore, it is an effective tactic for a home remodeler to go out into the area to meet people. He could leave a card and maybe a brochure with those he contacts. The home remodeler's goal is not an immediate sale. He or she is working to build trust, which should result in future projects.

Canvassing doesn't have to be door to door. Any action taken to meet potential customers face to face is canvassing. Civic groups and country clubs are also places to meet customers face to face. Don't try to give too polished a sales pitch when trying to win trust. What counts is eye contact, listening skills, and sincerity. You must be yourself to be sincere.

Canvassing is hard work. Many people, especially professionals, feel uncomfortable canvassing, but canvassing is worth the effort. Customers will go out of their way to deal with someone they trust.

MAXIMIZING THE EFFORTS OF YOUR DISTRIBUTION CHANNEL

Distribution Channel Changes

Your marketing thrust may call for a change in your distribution network. You may want to add distributors, eliminate distributors, or reorient them. As an example, National Semiconductor dropped distributors who carried a competitive product line; it wanted only distributors who supported the company's product exclusively. You may also want to alter your distributors' performance objectives as part of your marketing thrust.

You may also have goals of increasing distributors' support by offering more incentives, such as co-op advertising campaigns or in-store promotional materials.

Or perhaps you want to change your marketing thrust at the distributor level from the store owners to the salesforce, or maybe even to their service people. This is a major change and calls for an action plan. In one industry I was involved with, service personnel were influential in the purchase decision. They were the only employees the eventual buyer really trusted. Therefore, we directed our promotions to the service department, giving them special incentives.

In many businesses, the distributors are simply order takers—they do not actively promote your or anyone else's product. You may decide to introduce a program that helps the distributor and his salespeople learn how to increase sales by being more aggressive in calling attention to your product. If you use distributors, always look for ways that you can work more closely with them to influence their actions.

Changes in Sales Technique or Strategy

Your new marketing thrust may require some changes in the methods used by your salesforce. One change could be to have the salespeople switch from selling only one or two products of your line to selling the total line. Another sale change is having the salesforce give sales training or service clinics, rather than relying on the distributor management. Another possiblity would be to give only qualified leads to the salesforce.

Other changes deal with altering salespeoples' territories. You could cut the number of distributors each salesperson contacts so he or she could work more closely with each distributor and have time to make calls with the distributor's salesforce.

Remember that any change in the salesforce directives must be carefully handled, not only from a marketing perspective, but also from the perspective of the salesforce's morale. The same can be said about distributors. Don't make changes without considering the distributor's or salesforce's reaction.

THINKING BIG—INTRODUCING NEW PROGRAMS

Momentum is a key survival tactic to every business. It's also crucial in determining the success of a new program. My experience is that a program won't be successful unless it's accepted as a winner at its introduction.

Many articles have been written about the importance of first impressions. People make snap judgments after, in many cases, only 30 seconds. Your salesforce, distributors, and customers make those same snap judgments, and once that judgment has been made, it's hard to change.

Most people think of advertising first when they think of a big campaign. Advertising does work, but other tactics can be just as effective. Noxell introduced Clarion cosmetics with a point-of-purchase display which helped customers pick out their best makeup colors. It was the largest display in many retail stores' cosmetic departments. To date, Noxell has installed over 30,000 displays (*Potentials in Marketing*, May 1988); that's getting a program off to a good start!

I once was saddled with the introduction of a complex dealer incentive program. For a big introduction, I used the following collateral materials to give the program a big start:

A slide rule chart. This chart listed the discounts a dealer would get for various-size package purchases.

A set of eight ad slicks with suggested retail prices. A co-op ad program helped the dealer use the ad slicks to promote the product to his or her customers.

Promotional posters for each store.

A special display discount program. It helped dealers afford to purchase a complete display of our products.

In addition, a two-month ad campaign helped support the program which ran for six months. The program was a success because it had a big start.

Recently, a retail gift shop added a huge selection of Oriental merchandise but didn't use an introduction program. I'm sure that over time customers will realize that the shop has Oriental merchandise, and its sales will increase. Many industrial companies also introduce a new product without fanfare and let its sales grow slowly. A slow-growth strategy can work.

I like a big introduction because I want my business to be viewed as a leader in the market. A leader has control of its business. It has both a defensible and profitable marketing position. To be a leader, you must always look like a winner. Using big introductions is one tactic that makes a company look like a winner.

Chapter 9

INSIDE-OUT MARKETING: BUILDING YOUR PROGRAM FROM THE GROUND UP

The secret to success for a business is getting repeat customers. The best way to ensure repeat customers is to build your marketing program from the ground up. I like to call this technique inside-out marketing. An example of the benefits of inside-out marketing is two churches in my neighborhood, each wanting to attract young families. One church ran a direct mail campaign, but it was unable to sustain an initial attendance increase because it didn't have programs developed for young families. The other church decided to develop a strong youth education program prior to its direct mail campaign. Its attendance increased 10 to 20 percent. The goal of inside-out marketing is to make every aspect of your business (the inside) project your marketing thrust to customers (the outside).

For example, doctors, dentists, lawyers, and accountants should watch their advertising and marketing programs carefully; it is crucial to protect their image as skilled, trustworthy professionals. Inside-out marketing can be profitable to all of them. In one instance, a young dentist purchased a declining practice. He began by firing the receptionist who believed her primary job was to collect money. He then redecorated his office and installed special equipment to make his older patients more comfortable. His practice was then built upon the referrals from satisfied patients.

Business Marketing magazine (July 1988, page 98) had an article about a health service company which saved $600,000 over a two-year period by concentrating on keeping its present accounts. The marketing cost for this company to replace the lost accounts would have been an additional $400,000. The profits from inside-out marketing can be substantial, and in most cases, it doesn't require extensive planning or expensive budgets. Inside-out marketing calls for, first, treating your customers the same way you would like to be treated and, second, making every aspect of your business reflect your marketing strategies.

I once had a disagreement with a manufacturing manager over the quality of our company's service. As an experiment, I asked our purchasing department manager what 10 supplier actions purchasing agents disliked most. It turned out that our company was guilty of 8 of the 10. Ask yourself, "Is this how I'd like to be treated?" when evaluating your business. Never say, "This is what other companies do." Observe how other businesses treat customers. When you notice inside-out marketing tactics you like, consider incorporating them into your business.

One of my pet peeves is walking into a store and having a salesperson ask, "Can I help you?" If I want help, I'll ask for it. I feel "Can I help you?" means someone is coming to pester me. I recently had two experiences in which sales clerks demonstrated inside-out marketing.

In a clothing store, the salesperson's opening statement to me was, "Sir, I think you would look very nice in brown. I have some new shirts I'd like to show you." I like this approach for two reasons: one, the salesperson had something to offer—a color that would look good on me; and two, the salesperson was enhancing the store's image as the store to visit if a person wants to dress right.

At Bloomingdale's, my wife was looking at men's cologne. The sales opening was, "Hi! Can I show you this year's hot new men's cologne?" Again, the sales clerk was offering something of interest while at the same time enhancing Bloomingdale's image as "the store in the know."

Both of these examples occurred in expensive stores. The management of each knew the need to convince the customer to spend money at its store. Every business needs to do the same. A store that is not exclusive might not need inside-out marketing to survive, but inside-out marketing will certainly help sales.

Every time I think of inside-out marketing, I remember the Camera Shop's slogan "The focus is on you." It's a great slogan to describe how each business should evaluate itself. For instance, a flower shop owner in Iowa strove to make the customer the focus of his marketing strategy. Therefore, when his store's location couldn't provide convenient customer parking, the owner moved his business to a vacant gas station with plenty of parking on a busy street. Business increased dramatically.

Every aspect of your business should be examined to see how it focuses on your customers' needs and how it communicates your marketing strategy. This chapter covers the following three areas:

1. Following the golden rule—treating customers the way you like to be treated.
2. Making every phase of your business count.
3. How professionals can use inside-out marketing.

FOLLOWING THE GOLDEN RULE—TREATING CUSTOMERS THE WAY YOU LIKE TO BE TREATED

Trust Your Customers

I had the responsibility of the customer service department in one of my marketing positions. I used to get calls from irate customers after they had experienced some serious problems with the company's product. I always asked the customer the same question: What can I do to solve this problem that will satisfy you? More than 90 percent of the time, people asked for much less than I was willing to offer. The requests of the other 10 percent were usually not too much more. No one in my company believed that this technique worked until they saw the dollar figures of how little I spent satisfying irate customers. And the customer *was* happy—after all, he or she had decided the settlement.

Building customers' trust is a two-way proposition: customers won't trust a company if they feel the company does not trust them. About 15 years ago, I read an article about a Neiman Marcus store in Dallas, Texas. A woman wanted to return an expensive dress. The sales clerk didn't want to take the dress back because it couldn't be resold and because she thought that the damage to the dress was due to the customer's neglect. One of the store's founders happened to walk by and graciously took the dress back. Why? He felt this good will gesture would result in the woman becoming a regular customer.

I know this policy might sound foolish to many readers, but since I read that story, I've regarded every problem with a customer as an opportunity to build good will. Some people have taken advantage of me, but on the whole, trusting customers has been a successful strategy.

Another example of how helpful it can be to trust your customers is the policy of returns at Sears. Sears accepts virtually any return from its catalog sales. I took back a pair of pants once because I didn't like how they looked on me. Sears took the pants back without a question. This policy of Sears builds the trust that keeps customers.

Therefore, don't be afraid to back up your product and give the customer a chance to return it. Trust your customers to be fair with you. Don't institute cumbersome rules to prevent a few customers from taking advantage of you. Stringent rules irritate your faithful customers and hurt your business.

Give Good Service

Recently some of my friends returned from a cruise with a long list of complaints. Some were related to service, such as:

- The person in charge of snorkeling equipment didn't know how to snorkel.
- There was a 45-minute wait in line for just about everything.
- The ship employees never knew what time announced events were to occur.
- The waiters were responsible for too many tables to give good service.

Our friends were convinced that because the ship was understaffed, the employees had more responsibilities than they could easily handle.

Management of this ship suffered from a poor service attitude. Often company management claims that it is committed to service and that any service problems are caused by employees. I believe service problems exist because management doesn't attempt to solve them.

When I started my first job in sales, I went to lunch with a 35-year-old plant manager. He mentioned to me that he had been promoted over several more experienced unit operators because he had raised his unit's efficiency rate from 72 percent to 86 percent. When I asked him how he had managed to do that, he told me it was easy—all he did was ask, "Why not?" For instance, when he first took over the unit, he was told he would not be able to raise the efficiency rate over 72 percent. The young plant engineer asked, "Why not?" When he solved that problem, he was up to a 75 percent efficiency rate and on his way to 86 percent.

You need the same attitude as that plant manager if you want to offer good service. You need to look for problems and then solve them one at a time.

When I encounter a customer service problem, I like to investigate its cause; often it is something which can be easily rectified. Once I was waiting in a long line at a K mart. Every register was open, but the lines were not moving. The problem appeared to be that each checkout clerk had to get a supervisor to approve checks and credit cards. The supervisor just couldn't keep up with the demand for her service.

When I reached the checkout clerk, I asked if there were usually two supervisors. He told me, "No, it's really not worth having two. One is enough unless the store is busy." The clerk's comment raises the question, "Why should employees care about service when management doesn't?" Management's careless attitude about service is reflected in every phase of a company's operation.

Quality

Japanese companies, as a rule, have cautious marketing campaigns. They do two things very well: first, they build products the customer wants, and second, they build products of superior quality.

Quality, like service, occurs only when employees believe their management is committed to it. A plant manager of a company I worked for always talked about quality, but the factory workers thought that the manager's emphasis on quality was insincere. Each employee had two or three stories about how the plant manager had at one time skimped on quality. Needless to say, the plant had a reputation of manufacturing products of inferior quality.

Keep Your Customers

The *Philadelphia Inquirer* (July 31, 1988) published a story about Philadelphia's 32 prenatal care centers. The story featured a caseworker who spent 10 hours a week talking to pregnant women about the prenatal service. The caseworker stated that she was pleased that in one year she was able to convince 18 women to use the prenatal clinics.

I couldn't understand why the caseworker was satisfied; I thought 18 women were extremely few for a year's work—especially when the article stated that the service was desperately needed. An acquaintance of mine lives in a neighborhood with a prenatal center and wasn't surprised by the low response. Why? She said, "Don, you just get tired of the runaround those government agencies give you."

The above is an illustration that people don't like to do business with organizations that offer poor service—even when that service is valuable. Examine your business from the customer's point of view and correct each problem that would annoy you if you were the customer. Once you do this, you will begin to keep your customers.

MAKING EVERY PHASE OF YOUR BUSINESS COUNT

Each Employee Is Responsible for Public Relations

Every customer's experience with a business should be positive. The best way to create this ideal is to expect every employee to add value to a customer's visit. An example of my point is found at Toys "R" Us, a toy store in Philadelphia. I have two children under 10 years of age, so I often shop at Toys "R" Us. Finding a specific toy can be a problem at some stores—but not at Toys "R" Us. I just ask a stock clerk for what I want, and the clerk leads me right to the toy. In most toy stores, the stock clerks feel their job is merely to keep the shelves stocked. At Toys "R" Us, the stock clerks not only keep the shelves stocked, they keep the customers happy.

The principle of each employee adding value to each customer contact becomes increasingly important for mid- and high-priced products. In fact, if you sell an expensive product, you don't want employees just to help customers, you want them to go out of their way to help.

I personally believe department stores lose many sales because they ignore this principle. When I walk into a large department store with fairly high-priced merchandise, I usually can't find someone to wait on me. Well, it's a fairly difficult decision to purchase something when I might be able to buy a similar item for less at another store. Although it's possible that the department store has high-quality merchandise or better product back-up, the store didn't have anyone there to tell me that.

Every customer contact with your business should be positive. That will only happen when every employee can offer value to a customer.

In-Store Layouts

As an example of an in-store layout using inside-out marketing, consider a record store which promotes itself as in tune with today's "hot music." The shop's in-store layout could feature eight top-selling albums. All of the music in these albums could be placed in a juke box so customers, for a quarter, could hear the song of their choice.

The store could also feature at least three up-and-coming albums chosen by various disc jockeys. Prominent displays of the picks could be featured in the front of the store. Or the displays could be albums recorded by local bands. The store would then be positioned as the place to learn about today's music scene.

Clothing stores' layouts often fail to use inside-out marketing. Usually a clothing store's strategy focuses on selling clothes that make a person "look great." The store enhances its strategy by placing mannequins dressed in "great looking" outfits around the store. But customers often have to hunt around racks, trying to assemble some of those same outfits. Some specialty clothing stores practice inside-out marketing by placing blouses, skirts, and sweaters together on the same rack. Although not all the clothes are the same type or made by the same manufacturer, they complement each other.

A store catering to a certain clientele should arrange its clothes in a way that customers can find a total outfit. Sometimes I even think a catalog approach would work effectively in a clothing store: display a great number of outfits and have customers ask for a pants number or a shirt number in their size.

In marketing, it is wise to remember that potential customers, for the most part, don't pay all that much attention to your efforts to attract them. The one time they do evaluate your store is when they have decided to buy something from you. The theme of your store should be easily noticed by anyone who enters.

Product Packaging, Invoicing, Customer Follow-Up

If your business is not a store, you can still exhibit your marketing slogan and logo through many customer contacts. You have your product package, customer invoice, delivery system, and most importantly, your product follow-up as ways to promote your slogan.

Customer Service

Your customers will have the most contact with your company through your sales and customer service departments. Most companies make sure that their salespeople know about new products and programs and how to promote them. But customer service is usually not updated. This is dangerous because a customer needs between 5 and 10 positive experiences to cancel out the effects of one bad customer service experience.

Include the customer service department in your marketing thrust for the year. You might even provide employees in customer service a different slogan each week with which to answer the phone. At the very least, make sure they know everything about your products and programs that the salespeople know.

Sales Brochures

Sales brochures are important for communicating your marketing strategy. Customers often research a product of interest from three to six months prior to making a purchase. Your brochure may be the only contact the customer has while he or she gathers information.

For example, an industrial engineer may be designing a new piece of assembly equipment for the automotive industry. The engineer needs to include three small precision motors in the final product to move a robotic arm. The engineer might request information from 15 different manufacturers when he begins the project. Over a six-month period, the engineer will probably narrow his choice of motors to those offered by three manufacturers. His choice, most likely, is made solely from the manufacturers' brochures.

Most brochures, especially from industrial companies, are ineffective in communicating a company's marketing thrust. This is the result of two conflicting goals:

1. Quickly and effectively communicate what the product is, the product's purpose, and the company's marketing thrust.
2. Describe the product's features in enough detail so customers will know if the product meets their needs.

In my opinion, most brochures contain enough technical data, but don't get the information across quickly enough.

There are three rules I like to follow when I am preparing a brochure which describes a product or program briefly, yet thoroughly:

1. In three seconds, the cover should tell the reader what the product is and its purpose.
2. In 10 seconds, the reader should know about the company's marketing strategy and why he or she should buy the product.
3. The brochure must explain sufficiently the features of the product so the reader can determine if it meets his or her needs.

Most brochures disregard the second rule. A customer might have 15 brochures to examine and will skim all 15 before deciding which ones to read in detail. A brochure must be able to survive the skimming process.

The most effective way I have found to communicate a message briefly is to have on each page a visually dominating image that clearly demonstrates an important point of the product. To be visually dominating, the image needs to occupy at least a third of the page or double page if the image is inside the brochure. Before finalizing the brochure, place the visually dominating images on a wall. Ask co-workers what message the images create. If they can identify the message, your brochure will be effective.

HOW PROFESSIONALS CAN USE
INSIDE-OUT MARKETING

Client trust is essential for a professional practice to succeed. I've seldom felt that advertising by a professional was helpful for generating trust, especially when professionals advertise low prices.

But the issue of professional advertising goes beyond the message itself; the physical appearance of the advertising also communicates a message. High-priced products use glossy attractive ads to convey a high-end image. If professionals advertise, their ads must reflect professionalism. They need a high-quality ad and brochure to communicate that they are competent and trustworthy. High-quality ads are expensive and typically are not cost justified for the professional's typical small target market.

A professional should use inside-out marketing to communicate three messages to his clients or patients:

1. I care about you.
2. I know what I'm doing.
3. You, as the client, have control.

Although virtually every reader will agree that it is important to communicate the first two messages, I expect many readers will be surprised at the last message—the client has control. After all, professionals have spent a long time preparing themselves for their fields. They know much more about their field than the client.

Consider the client's point of view. He or she has a lot at stake when seeing a professional. The client needs to believe that the services offered are competent and in his or her best interest.

How does the professional communicate to the client or patient that he or she is getting the most appropriate professional advice? I believe it comes from a professional discussing with the client or patient the problem, its causes, and the options available to correct the problem. The professional lets the client or patient share in the analysis of the problem and in the knowledge of why the professional has chosen one course of action over another.

My wife provides an example of what happens when a professional doesn't communicate with a client. She had just returned from the dentist's office and told me she needed a crown costing $450.00. When I asked why, she said, "Something is wrong with the tooth." I asked if there were any other possible treatments besides the crown. "I don't know," she answered. "The dentist just said I needed a crown."

Because my wife failed to be assertive in asking for more information, the result of this visit was that my wife and I were not sure that this dentist's suggested treatment was the best or only solution to the problem.

It is important for professionals to recognize that their clients will have buyer's remorse—the point when a buyer begins to think a purchase is a poor choice. Salespeople know that the way to overcome buyer's remorse is to supply buyers with a great deal of information about their purchase. Professionals also need to provide clients with enough information to avoid buyer's remorse.

How does a professional use the inside-out marketing strategy? The rest of this section describes various tactics the professional can use to communicate those three important messages: I care about you; I know what I'm doing; and you have control.

I Care About You

Numerous articles have been written about the need for professionals to project a warm, friendly "I care" attitude from the first moment a patient or client enters the office. This is accomplished by the friendliness and concern of every staff member, as well as the comfort and attractiveness of the office. Professionals also need to start an appointment with a short, friendly conversation with a client or patient. Not only does this indicate an interest in the client, but it helps the client to relax and feel more comfortable.

Some of the steps that express caring are practiced by the professionals I use. I like my dentist because his office staff always lets me know when he is running behind schedule and will be late for my appointment. I like my doctor because he takes appointments on two evenings a week and on Saturday mornings. I like my ophthalmologist because during my eye examinations, he always explains what he is doing and why.

Professionals use other tactics which are appropriate for their practices. If professionals want to know of other things they can do to express this attitude of caring, they should ask their staffs. Often they have more contact with clients and can pinpoint areas where the professional can show the client a caring attitude.

I Know What I'm Doing

I discussed in Chapter 4 (pages 63–65) the importance of placement strategies for professionals in projecting an "I know what I'm doing" image. A doctor should have an office in a medical complex. A lawyer should have an office in a professional building.

A professional also needs to ensure that every experience a client or patient has while in his office communicates the message that "this professional is an expert."

In the reception room there should be an ample supply of current literature on topics of interest to the clients or patients. For example, a doctor might have a pamphlet "How to Prevent Heart Attacks" in his reception room. By sharing new information that is pertinent to the patient, the professional demonstrates the importance he or she places on education. That helps the client feel that the professional knows what he or she is doing.

A local lawyer has a great reception strategy. After clients check in at the reception desk, they are escorted to the law firm's library where law books line the walls and magazines are out in racks. The client can't help but feel the lawyers know what they are doing.

Another tactic professionals can use to project an "I know what I'm doing" image is to take time to listen to the client.

As an example of what happens when a professional doesn't listen, imagine that you hired me as a consultant for your business. When I arrived, I walked around your office for a couple of minutes, talked to a few employees, and then told you that there were some serious problems with your marketing strategies. What would your reaction be? You would probably be thinking, "Who is this guy?" After all, you have been in practice for five years; you've read many marketing articles; and you've done a great deal of research on how to create an effective marketing program. And here I am, ready to tell you what to do after only a few minutes. You are likely to think that I haven't a clue about how to properly market your business. Clients and patients will feel the same way about professionals who don't take the time to listen to and examine their problems.

Explaining to the patient or client what is going to be done, how, and why, implies that the professional knows what he or she is doing. On my last visit to the dentist, the dental hygienist never explained anything. The dentist, on the other hand, explained everything he was doing and why. Those explanations increased my confidence in the dentist.

When I had the responsibility of the customer service department for a company, customers (in this example, the customers were dealers) told me that our company provided very poor service and that the management didn't know what it was doing. Our major competitor, the customers claimed, provided excellent service, and its management was knowledgeable and efficient. When I did a little research to discover how much better our competitor's service was, I was amazed to find that our late shipments and lead times were almost identical.

The difference between customers' perception of the two companies was due to the competitor's policy of always notifying the customer about a late shipment; the competitor kept the customer informed. On the other hand, our company never informed a customer of a delayed shipment. When we changed our policy, our customers began to perceive the company as one that knew what it was doing.

The Client Has Control

Customers like to feel in control of the purchasing process. They like to believe that they have researched the various purchasing options and have chosen the best one. The customers' desire for control of the purchasing process is an important marketing aspect that professionals should focus on.

I want to make it clear before continuing that I don't mean that the professional should let the client or patient dictate the professional's strategy, but the client or patient does need to know the pros and cons of each available option. The client can then appreciate and agree with the professional's choice of strategies. If the client chooses an option that's unacceptable to the professional, the professional can refuse to accept that patient or client.

Non-HMO physicians in Minnesota provide a good example of how the strategy of letting the client have control can be an effective marketing tactic.

In Minnesota, HMOs are popular, providing serious competition for non-HMO physicians. Non-HMO physicians claim they offer better medical care than the HMO physicians because HMO physicians can offer only low-cost medical treatments which may or may not be the best treatment for the patient.

The non-HMO physicians need to differentiate their services from HMO physicians with a strategy of putting the patient in control. Non-HMO physicians should promote the fact that the patient's condition and all the treatment options available will be discussed with the patient and that patients will be offered the best treatment.

I've mentioned several times that I think professionals need to be cautious with any advertising strategy. I feel price-oriented or poor-quality advertising detracts from a professional's image. Nevertheless, a carefully planned ad campaign that implies concern for the patient can reinforce the physician's image as skilled and competent.

I asked one physician why he was reluctant to discuss treatment options with his patients. He said that he was concerned that his patients would worry too much if they knew everything that could go wrong with a treatment plan. For some patients, this may be a wise decision, but

I think most patients today are more concerned about their health when they don't know what their options are.

Letting your customer know that he or she is in control of his or her relationship with you is a good tactic for every business, including a professional one.

SUMMARY

Most of the tactics mentioned in this chapter are inexpensive. In this book, I have stressed consistency. Consistency does not occur just from running the same ad campaign; it comes from using a total approach, from having every employee and every facet of a business reflect the same marketing thrust.

While inside-out marketing may not be as expensive as advertising, it is the most difficult marketing tactic to implement. You can't hire an outsider to do this job; you have to do it yourself. It may require that you re-evaluate some practices that have been company policy for years.

PART 2 SUMMARY

Now you should be able to list the tactics you want to implement in your marketing thrust. You also need to estimate the cost of each tactic on the list.

The total cost of your proposed marketing tactics will most likely exceed the amount budgeted. In Chapter 2 (pages 21–23), the compromise decision model was discussed to evaluate how a customer can decide which product to purchase. You can use the same model to determine which tactics you will incorporate into your market plan. Reorganize your list of tactics into: must have; important to have; and nice to have strategies. Finally measure the cost of each tactic against its importance before selecting the tactics you will use. It may turn out you can't run some "important-to-have" programs because of their costs, while you can run some low-cost "nice-to-have" programs.

Remember that it is better to execute a few tactics well than to execute many tactics poorly. Budget enough money on each tactic to make it effective.

For an example of how to use the compromise model to choose marketing tactics, consider a non-HMO physician in Minnesota.

Non-HMO Physician—Tactics Selection Chart

	Cost	Rating	To Be Used?
Must-Have Tactics			
Explain treatment options to all patients.	0	10	Yes
Have a consultant train the staff to be friendly and to project an "I know what I'm doing" image.	$ 2,000	10	Yes
Order patient-information pamphlets from the American Medical Association.	$ 1,500	10	Yes
Important-to-Have Tactics			
Remodel a room for effective patient con-sultations.	$ 3,000	7	Yes
Write, with the help of a copy-writer, a pamphlet about how the non-HMO physi-cian views patients' rights.	$ 3,500	5	No
Attend a seminar on "Physicians for Patients' Rights" to learn how to discuss medical options with patients.	$ 995	6	Yes
Join "Physicians for Patients' Rights" asso-ciation. Membership includes an advertis-ing program.	$10,000	4	No
Run a direct mail cam-paign in the local area.	$ 6,000	5	No
Give talks at schools and local civic groups to explain how the physician views patients' rights.	0	3	Yes

PART 3

WRITING THE MARKETING PLAN

You write a marketing plan for four major reasons:

It forces you to sit down and evaluate your business or product periodically. Otherwise, marketers can miss significant trends that may be developing in their business.

It is a document that can be read by someone else in your company or an investor that explains your marketing strategy.

It is a document with a specific timetable that provides a reference for you to follow throughout the year. The timetable helps keep you on schedule and provides a listing of your marketing expenses for a year. This expense budget tells you if you can afford your marketing plan.

It is a document that will allow someone new to come in and take over the marketing activities. The new person should be able to understand what key marketing elements a plan focuses on and when each planned tactic is scheduled to be implemented.

The marketing plan contains two contradictory elements. First, it should be brief enough to provide quick and easy reading for people who just want to know the essence of your marketing activities. Second, the plan should be specific with an action timetable. The marketing plan meets both objectives by containing a brief overview of the rationale behind the strategy at the front of the plan and a detailed timetable at the end of the plan.

Chapter 10 lays out the marketing plan format and explains the purpose for each item in the plan. Chapters 11–13 contain marketing plans for eight businesses. The eight plans cover a wide variety of situations and each attacks a different marketing problem. Read all the plans before coming back to Chapter 10 to write your own plan. Some of the businesses in the plans may not be similar to yours, but I recommend that you read every plan as each one offers a marketing approach that could be used in a wide variety of businesses.

The first two plans are based on McDonald's and Hitachi VCRs. These are not the actual plans those two companies use, but rather my impression of what their plans might look like. The sales dollars and market share data are not accurate. I've chosen to use McDonald's because the company's marketing moves are known to most people and because, even though McDonald's is successful, it too has marketing problems to deal with. I chose Hitachi because I have mentioned its marketing problems several times in the book, including using Hitachi as the example for the marketing plan checklist.

Five of the last six marketing plans are not based on real companies, but they are based on real problems companies face. The marketing plans were created to give the reader exposure to a variety of marketing problems and solutions. The other plan is based on The Paper Outlet, the store discussed in Chapter 7 (page 117).

Keep in mind as you read the marketing plans that every marketing problem has several possible solutions. You may have another effective solution to a company's marketing problem than the one discussed in the plan. Don't be afraid to use your own solution.

Always think of consistency when you write a marketing plan. If your company has successfully used a marketing tactic in the past, consider using it again. Customers relate easily to a consistent marketing approach. Don't be afraid to change your approach if it's not working, but don't change just for the sake of change.

CHAPTER 10

THE MARKETING PLAN FORMAT

1. Objectives

Sales dollars   _____
Gross profit dollars   _____
Gross margin percent   _____
Net profit dollars   _____
Dollar market share   _____

This opening section gives a quick capsule view of a product's sales objectives and position. A description of each item follows:

Sales dollars. This figure represents your expected sales for the next year.

Gross profit dollars. This is your sales dollars less the cost to buy or produce your product. Gross profit dollars tells a reader how much money a product is contributing toward sales, advertising, and administrative expenses.

Gross margin percent. Gross margin percent is calculated by dividing the gross profit dollars by the sales dollars. Most industries have a typical gross margin percent. For example, the pharmaceutical industry has an average gross margin percent of about 80 percent. Heavy equipment manufacturers have a gross margin percent of about 45 percent. This figure varies among industries. The gross margin percent tells you how a product's profitability compares to the industry norm.

Net profit dollars. This figure is your gross profit dollars less marketing, sales, administrative, and overhead expenses. This number tells you if a product is making money. If a company has several products, this information may not be available for each product. If not, omit this number.

Dollar market share. Dollar market share tells a reader how important you are in the market. If you don't have market share data, try to estimate it. Refer to Chapter 6 (pages 96–97) for examples of how to estimate market share.

2. Sales History

	Last Three Years			Next Two Years	
	1986	1987	1988	1989	1990
Total market dollar size	——	——	——	——	——
Your dollar sales	——	——	——	——	——
Dollar market size	——	——	——	——	——

The last three years should be your actual sales history. The next two years are your estimate of what sales will be.

If you don't have a sales history, this section should explain how you predicted your first-year sales. If your business is similar to another, you can use its sales volume. For example, my wife and I liked the educational toys in a Philadelphia toy store. We considered opening a similar store in Minneapolis, so we found out the Philadelphia store's sales volume as well as the number of mall visitors per day. We found a mall in Minneapolis in a similar neighborhood with similar mall traffic. But my wife noticed that fewer mall visitors in Minneapolis made purchases than in Philadelphia. It turned out to be 25 percent fewer; therefore, we projected our first year's sales volume at 75 percent of the Philadelphia store's volume.

If you don't have a similar store, it's more difficult to explain a projected sales volume, but it can be done. I recently worked on the introduction of a unique piece of electronic assembly equipment. We had people evaluate a prototype unit, and they all raved about it. When I had to determine the first year's sales volume, here are the steps I took:

I estimated the potential market size from industry sources and magazine articles. There were about 3,000 potential customers, and each could buy two to five units for an estimated market size of approximately 7,000 units.

I researched how many units of the equipment we would be partially replacing had been sold over the last three years. About 950 units had been sold, 400 in the last year. Sales projections for the next year were 700 units.

I examined first-year sales of other equipment products that had been introduced to our potential customers. Usually successful new products sold between 200 and 400 units.

I researched potential customers and found that about 35 percent of the prospects would prefer our equipment to the equipment we would be replacing.

My final sales projection was 225 to 250 units, based on 700 potential units times 35 percent or 245 units. This number was also consistent with past introductions of new products to the industry.

3. Market Share Trends

	Last Three Years			Next Two Years	
	1986	1987	1988	1989	1990
Your market share	——	——	——	——	——
1st major competitor	——	——	——	——	——
2nd major competitor	——	——	——	——	——
3rd major competitor	——	——	——	——	——
4th major competitor	——	——	——	——	——
Others	——	——	——	——	——

Chapter 6 (pages 94–96) discussed in depth a market trend analysis for a dental delivery unit. The value of market share trends is that they indicate how you are doing compared to the competition. They also point out which competitor may be rapidly increasing market share.

If you don't have accurate market share data, try to estimate your market share. Chapter 6 (pages 96–97) gives two examples of estimating market share.

4. Commentary

This section should give an overview of the events that occurred over the last year or two, leading to your current market position. List major events, trends, and competitive developments that have either happened or are expected to happen. This section should identify the key marketing elements the plan will address.

5. Competition

This section should list your major competitors and how you judge their current position, including any significant strengths or weaknesses.

Also consider complementary products as competitors if they are a factor in your business. For example, if you are in a mall selling athletic shoes, consider a sporting goods store that sells shoes as a competitor. Or if you sell a word processing system, consider a low-cost computer with word processing capabilities as a competitor.

6. Price Comparison/Price Value

This section contains a price comparison chart with your and your competitors' prices. After you list the prices, you may want to note any significant features that explain the price differences, such as one color TV doesn't have remote control, accounting for its lower price. Also list subjective features such as product quality if it's an area of significant difference between competitors.

The prices listed should be a net price after promotional discounts. For example, if your average price after discounts is $75 and the posted price is $100 you should list the $75 price.

In the last part of this section, list any planned routine price increases. Any significant price adjustments, for positioning purposes, should be listed in the tactics section.

7. Problems/Opportunities

This section contains a brief description of your problems and opportunities. Include both short- and long-term problems. This is the part of the plan you come back to when you're finished to ask yourself the questions: Have I addressed the problems and opportunities? Does the plan address meaningful marketing elements? Does the plan have enough impact in the critical areas? Have I overlooked any important points?

8. Major Thrusts

This section contains the major thrusts you will implement in the next year. The format requires you list first the thrust, making it clear what key marketing element or problem area you are focusing on, and second, in broad terms, the tactics you will be using.

For instance, in the McDonald's example, the first thrust listed is: Continue to foster children's loyalty to McDonald's.

- Run commercials with Ronald McDonald during children's programs.
- Continue to run Happy Meal promotions.
- Continue expansion of McDonald's playlands.

This section is designed to capture quickly what you are trying to accomplish and how you plan to do it. Your purpose here is in responding to the market position you described in Sections 4 and 7.

There may be situations where a marketing plan cannot resolve every problem, capitalize on every opportunity, or focus on every key marketing element. You should add an explanation in this section of why you didn't focus on certain areas and when you will address them.

For example, you may be a struggling manufacturer of industrial equipment. Your marketing situation includes:

- Your specialized salesforce is the wrong placement strategy.
- Your price/value relationship is too high.
- You have poor name recognition.
- Your greatest strength is in a shrinking market segment.

Your marketing plan might be able to focus on the last three issues this year; then next year you will start to realign your placement strategy.

9. Minor Thrusts

This section contains the minor steps you might be taking next year, such as introducing a new dealer contract, changing a product's packaging, or introducing new sales tools. Listing these here fills out the marketing plan so it includes all of your marketing efforts.

10. Positioning Statement

Chapter 8 (pages 140–141) discussed positioning statements which describe how your company views a product or service. For example, your positioning statement might be that you provide all the office supplies lawyers need; that you are a neighborhood record store that caters to teenagers; or that you supply an elegant sports car for high-income professionals.

Your positioning statement is not your marketing slogan. A marketing slogan conveys a message to the customer. A positioning statement is for internal company use. It makes it clear to every employee what the company is trying to accomplish. It's listed in the marketing plan because you want to be sure the marketing plan supports the company's positioning statement. In some cases, a company will be changing a positioning statement. Be sure to explain any changes in this section.

11. Tactics

List in detail all the tactics you plan to implement. As a reminder, I've listed below some of the tactics you may want to use:

Ad campaigns	Packaging strategy
Promotional programs	Market research
In-store promotions	Changes in sales strategy
Sales literature	Store displays and layouts
Sales aids	Window displays
Sales meetings	Store signs
Salesforce newsletters	Customer service
Name changes	Distributor newsletters
Marketing slogans	Placement strategy changes
Public relations	Distributor support materials
Direct mail	Canvassing
Conventions	Significant price changes
Inside-out marketing	Any other major effort

You may have prepared a thorough analysis for some tactics. If so, you should give a brief description of the tactic in the marketing plan and then add the analysis as an attachment.

12. Where Will the Business Come From?

This section justifies your sales projections. For example, if your sales projections in the first section of the plan call for a 20 percent increase, you should explain how your marketing thrust and tactics will generate a 20 percent increase.

Consider a car wash whose sales projection calls for a 50 percent sales increase. Its marketing thrust is to convince neighborhood residents that the car wash does a better job than they can do at home. The car wash's tactics include adding a larger, more noticeable sign, buying whitewall tire cleaning equipment, and increasing advertising in local newspapers to once a week.

The car wash manager had taken a survey of the neighborhood people who didn't use the car wash and found that people felt they could get their cars as clean as the car wash could. Five percent of the people surveyed said they would use the car wash if they thought the car wash could do a better job. That 5 percent of the neighborhood would double the car wash's business, so the owner felt that promoting his new whitewall service would get half the potential 5 percent to be customers.

Does this plan make sense?—no, a whitewall cleaning service is not that attractive. Often a marketing plan lists a series of sound tactics that just don't have enough impact to reach a plan's sales objectives.

This is the one section of the marketing plan format that is different than most other published formats. I like it because it forces you to prove your sales objectives are reasonable and obtainable. I've changed many plans because they don't pass the "where will the business come from" test.

13. Timetable

This section lists a timetable to refer to throughout the year. It also allows you to determine marketing costs on a monthly basis. A format that should be used is:

Action Items	Key Dates	Quantity	Costs	Person Responsible
_____	_____	_____	_____	_____
_____	_____	_____	_____	_____
_____	_____	_____	_____	_____

The key dates are the months a program will be implemented. Some programs may have several key dates, such as an ad campaign that may need to be introduced to dealers a month before its general release. In this case, note both dates in the timetable.

The format also includes a column for the person responsible for implementing the program. I did not include this column in any of the plans in the following chapters, but if you have several people working on marketing activities, prevent confusion by listing who is responsible for each program's implementation.

14. Key Risks

What are the key risks of your plan? You want to be aware of any problems that might come up and force you to adjust your marketing plan. Major key risks could include:

Your marketing plan depends on certain assumptions which may not be correct.

A competitor may release a product earlier than expected.

Your plan may not have enough impact to achieve the plan's ambitious sales growth goals.

Your new features are unique, and customer acceptance is based on market studies and not actual buyer behavior.

A competitor has been recently acquired. New management may rejuvenate the company.

Your marketing plan is based on a successful plan in another market. Your market may not respond in the same way as the other market.

You may have key risks other than these. List any risk you feel your marketing plan has. Always ask yourself if every risk is acceptable. In particular, avoid large risks on your lead product.

This format is designed to cover all the important points of a marketing plan. In some cases, parts of the format won't apply to your business. For example, a professional does not have to worry about gross margins; professionals are interested in what percentage of the gross they take home. I've modified the marketing plans in Chapters 11–13 where appropriate.

CHAPTER 11

MARKETING PLANS OF SUCCESSFUL COMPANIES

The first marketing plan in this chapter belongs to McDonald's. McDonald's has an extremely consistent marketing strategy with several strong elements: the golden arches and Ronald McDonald, effective visual images; a consistent emphasis on children, which has developed the restaurant's loyal customer base; periodic menu changes, which have helped McDonald's keep adult customers; and a steady increase in outlets, generating the funding for McDonald's to outpromote competition.

Every year the McDonald's strategy has been the same, and that consistency has made it successful. But now McDonald's is running out of places to put new outlets, and it's struggling to hold market share among adults.

This market plan is an example of how I feel McDonald's might react to its marketing situation. The sales and market share numbers are not actual sales, though they are reasonably close. The McDonald's marketing plan is an example of using marketing strengths to deal with current problems.

The second study in this chapter is a Hitachi market plan. Hitachi has done well in the VCR market primarily because the market grew rapidly. It placed its VCRs primarily through discount TV and stereo stores and has been successful in those outlets because of its low price and promotional discounts. Now the VCR market is mature, and competitors are fighting for market share. Hitachi must improve its marketing position to survive in the VCR market.

Again, this plan is my view of a potential Hitachi marketing plan. The numbers are not accurate, though they are representative. Hitachi's marketing plan is an example of a company trying to establish a defensible position in a competitive market.

1989—POSSIBLE McDONALD'S MARKETING PLAN

1. Objectives

Sales dollars	$12 billion
Gross profit dollars	$4.3 billion
Gross margin percent	36%
Net profit dollars	$1.3 billion
Dollar market share	25.5%

Note: These objectives consolidate sales numbers for McDonald's-owned outlets, affiliates, and franchises.

2. Sales History

	1986	1987	1988	1989	1990
Total dollar market size	$44.0	$44.0	$45.0	$47.0	$51.0
McDonald's dollar sales	11.0	11.1	11.4	12.0	13.1
McDonald's market share	25.0%	25.2%	25.3%	25.5%	25.7%

All sales are in billions.

3. Market Share Trends

	1986	1987	1988	1989	1990
McDonald's	25.0%	25.2%	25.3%	25.5%	25.7%
Burger King	9.6	9.5	9.6	9.5	9.5
Wendy's	5.4	5.7	5.8	5.8	5.8
Hardee's	5.5	5.6	5.7	5.7	5.7
Chicken outlets	18.4	18.6	18.7	18.7	18.8
Taco outlets	7.5	7.5	7.3	7.4	7.4

4. Commentary

The fast-food market is growing slowly. The traditional neighborhood and suburban markets are saturated, and most current sales growth is from nontraditional outlets, such as airport, railroad depot, and office building locations.

The fast-food industry is still centered around hamburger, chicken, and taco outlets. Some newer specialty outlets, for example D'Lites, offer more adult menu choices, such as pasta bars. These outlets pose a potential threat to McDonald's as they are focused on singles and adults without children, market segments with little loyalty to McDonald's.

Along with the emergence of specialty chains, new chicken outlets such as Popeye's and improved marketing efforts by Kentucky Fried Chicken continue to pressure hamburger outlets. On the positive side, both Wendy's and Burger King have been running weak promotional campaigns.

A summary of positive and negative events of the last few years follows:

Positive events:

- Successful introduction of salads and the McDLT sandwich.
- The continued demand from children for Happy Meals.
- McDonald's playgrounds are successfully increasing outlet sales.
- Continued domination by McDonald's of the fast-food breakfast market.

Negative events:

- Slow growth in the fast-food market.
- Diminishing loyalty to McDonald's in the nonchildren market.
- Competitors have introduced versions of Happy Meals.
- New outlet locations are becoming more difficult to find.
- Recent nutritional reports on McDonald's products have been negative.

Two major issues face McDonald's: first, how does it increase loyalty among adults without modifying its traditionally strong emphasis on children? and second, how does it keep up its market momentum when new outlet locations are increasingly difficult to find?

People's loyalty to McDonald's has always declined as they grow older. Adults switch from one fast-food chain to another when a new food item is available. The introduction of the McDLT, and before that Chicken McNuggets, has held the restaurant's market share with the adult market segment. Another factor that has helped McDonald's keep adults' business is the failure of Burger King and Wendy's to introduce any new products.

McDonald's has tried to increase adult loyalty with an ad campaign featuring Tom Poston and a Big Mac attack. Though the ad tested well, it didn't produce appreciable results. Ads apparently aren't effective in changing the customer's image of McDonald's well-known products.

The second major issue McDonald's faces is how to keep up market momentum after saturating the market. McDonald's has few potential locations where opening a new outlet won't hurt an existing one. Burger King, with half as many outlets as McDonald's, and Wendy's, with a third as many, have been able to hold market share despite lackluster marketing performances by opening a greater percentage of new outlets.

Hardee's also has aggressive expansion plans into markets where it is weak, with real growth potential in some major markets. For example, in the Philadelphia area, Hardee's has only six outlets.

McDonald's has been able to hold market share by outspending its competitors on advertising and promotion. McDonald's spends roughly $700 million compared to Burger King's $200 million. This has kept McDonald's sales per store higher than any competitor's.

One factor in McDonald's favor is that the competitors are having trouble remaining profitable while expanding. Nevertheless, every new competitive outlet makes it more difficult for McDonald's sales to keep increasing.

McDonald's has been able to successfully expand overseas, but those outlets won't help U.S. market momentum as the number of competitive outlets grow.

5. Competition

Burger King. Burger King has stumbled badly over the last few years. Its advertising programs have been ineffective, and Burger King has not introduced any significant new products. Burger King's only positive moves have been to copy McDonald's Happy Meals and to upgrade its breakfast menus.

Wendy's. Wendy's is also struggling. It lost its marketing momentum when it dropped the effective "Where's the beef?" program. Wendy's has not added new menu items, and it's unclear how profitable its outlets can be.

Kentucky Fried Chicken. Kentucky Fried Chicken is in the process of upgrading its outlets. It is also adding sandwiches to its menu, and its advertising slogan "We do chicken right" is effective. McDonald's expects Kentucky Fried Chicken to continue to upgrade its outlets. Once Kentucky Fried Chicken converts enough outlets, it will probably launch a major advertising program.

D'Lites. While D'Lites is not a major competitor, it represents a concept that could hurt McDonald's. D'Lites appeals to adults with a pasta bar and salad menu that is especially popular at lunchtime. It offers what adults perceive as a more nutritional menu. Although D'Lites is poorly financed and is having cash flow problems, many of its individual stores are doing well.

Taco Bell. Taco Bell as well as other taco restaurants have carved out a niche market of people who like an occasional Mexican meal. Taco Bell has not grown to the size where it can advertise extensively. Also, tacos' appeal to a small number of customers restricts taco outlets to large cities and the southwest regional market.

6. Price Comparison

	Low-Priced Meals	Mid-Range Meals	Top-of-the-Line Meals
McDonald's	$2.10	$3.25	$4.10
Burger King	2.05	3.10	4.00
Wendy's	N/A	3.25	4.25
Kentucky Fried Chicken	N/A	3.50	4.65
Taco Bell	1.70	2.90	4.50
D'Lites	N/A	3.70	5.25

Note: N/A—Not available.

Although there are price differences between competitors, larger meal size or a fancier menu item justifies the price premiums that exist. Customers perceive a similar price/value relationship for all fast-food competitors and choose fast-food restaurants by taste preferences or location rather than price.

McDonald's will increase prices 3 to 5 percent in July 1989.

7. Problems/Opportunities

Problems:

1. Customers, in field tests, have not given high ratings to any of McDonald's potential new food items.
2. The number of potential locations for new McDonald's outlets is limited.
3. D'Lites has demonstrated the potential for an adult-oriented fast-food chain.
4. Competitors have introduced versions of the Happy Meal. Wendy's has run one successful Happy Meal-type promotion with Potato Head toys.
5. McDonald's last two game promotions, which were targeted to adults, were unsuccessful. Market surveys indicate customers thought the games were too complicated.
6. Food and service quality are starting to decline due to both the difficulty in hiring qualified workers and the difficulty in keeping up quality with an expanding menu.

Opportunities:

1. Market surveys indicate that McDonald's would receive a positive response to optional whole wheat buns.
2. McDonald's outlets in nontraditional locations are successful.
3. Marketing capabilities of McDonald's regional cooperatives, groups of local franchises, are the best in the industry.
4. McDonald's salad introduction has been moderately successful.
5. Every fast-food chain's products are being criticized by nutritional experts.

8. Major Thrusts

McDonald's is in a year of uncertainty; it doesn't have any new products to hold onto the adult market this year, nor will it be able to match its competitors' percentage growth of outlets. McDonald's is currently preparing to test market several new concepts that would satisfy both customers who like traditional McDonald's food and those who are looking for a menu change.

This year McDonald's goal is to hold market share with a product line unchanged except for the addition of whole wheat buns in selected markets. The major thrusts to achieve this goal are:

1. Continue strong marketing programs directed toward children.

   Run commercials featuring Ronald McDonald on children's programs.

   Continue to run Happy Meal promotions.

   Continue to increase the number of McDonald's playlands.

2. Target promotions at the adult market segment.

   Run a game promotion every six months.

   Introduce whole wheat buns in urban areas in the Northeast and on the West Coast. Advertise the whole wheat option with a radio ad campaign.

   Test market several new concepts that might develop stronger customer loyalty among adults.

   Return the double cheeseburger, a popular menu item of the 1960s, to the menu in the fall. Advertising will focus on "growing up with McDonald's."

3. Continue to add outlets in nontraditional locations.

9. Minor Thrusts

1. Expand the number of support materials available for regional cooperatives' use in their ad campaigns.
2. Expand the number of McDonald's-sponsored sports events.
3. Increase the number of Ronald McDonald appearances.
4. Issue press releases regarding the nutritional content of McDonald's food.

10. Positioning Statement

McDonald's is a fast-food restaurant that caters to both families and adults for breakfast, lunch, and dinner. McDonald's will offer a variety of menu choices though hamburgers will be featured. McDonald's intends to modify its menu and expand locations to serve the changing tastes of its customers.

11. Tactics

Ad Campaigns. McDonald's will continue to outspend its nearest competitor by a three- or four-to-one ratio, capitalizing on its large market share. The plan emphasizes two programs:

1. Children-oriented ads will run on children's TV shows. Ads will feature Happy Meal promotions, McDonald's playlands, and Ronald McDonald.
2. Adult-oriented ad campaigns will be run on evening and weekend TV programs and on adult radio programs. The campaigns by quarter are:

1st quarter: Advertise an adult-oriented game promotion.

2nd quarter: Introduce campaign announcing the addition of optional whole wheat buns in targeted cities. "It's a good time for the great taste of McDonald's" ads will run in nontargeted markets.

3rd quarter: Advertise another adult-oriented game promotion.

4th quarter: Introduce the nostalgia campaign of "growing up with McDonald's" with a three-month reintroduction of the double cheeseburger.

Promotional Strategy. Although McDonald's last two promotions initially increased sales, sales quickly returned to normal levels. Surveys indicate that customers thought the promotions were too complicated.

Success in the game promotions is crucial this year; promotions must pick up the potential drop in sales due to the absence of any major menu changes. The programs must be much simpler than the last ones. The game promotion ad campaign also needs to focus on game rules. Adult customers are not willing to take the time to learn the rules while eating.

McDonald's has hired a special promotion consulting firm to help devise a contest with simple rules. Three possible contests are being tested with small groups of customers. The game that has received high scores from consumers features both instant food prizes and chances for major prizes, including overseas trips and automobiles. This promotion is currently being scheduled for release in the first quarter.

In-Restaurant Promotions. McDonald's will continue to offer Happy Meals with a monthly theme change. The price for McDonald's playlands will decrease 35 percent to encourage outlet playground purchases.

Restaurant Displays. Major displays featuring banners and large posters are planned both for the game promotions and for the introduction of whole wheat buns. Poster holders will be available for mounting posters to condiment tables and trash receptacles.

Public Relations. Three public relations campaigns are planned this year:

1. McDonald's will offer continued support of various contests around the country, including golf and tennis tournaments, high school all-star games, and high school band competitions.
2. Each regional cooperative will be asked to double the number of Ronald McDonald appearances in its area. McDonald's will help fund this additional expense.
3. Articles will be released about the introduction of nutritional whole wheat buns to counter articles about the poor nutritional content of McDonald's foods.

Packaging Strategy. More nutritional information will be placed on food packaging to enhance McDonald's image as a healthy place to eat.

Market Research. Market research on both new food items and alternative placement strategies will be conducted.

1. Market research activities for new food items:

   • Run an employee contest, offering a free trip to Europe for the three best suggestions for new food items.
   • Test market the three winning food items.

2. Test market various new placement options:

- Test new restaurant layouts where one half of the outlet is family oriented and the other half adult oriented.
- Test the possibility of modifying the menu at 7 P.M. to be more adult oriented.
- In large cities, test the concept of using hand delivery carts to office complexes at lunchtime.

Regional Cooperatives Strategy. New support materials will be offered to regional cooperatives for their ad programs. In addition, a three-person creative team will be available to help regional cooperatives design their own promotional strategy.

Outlet Strategy. McDonald's will continue to add outlets and franchises in the following areas:

- Promising overseas countries.
- Nontraditional locations.
- Growing or resurging neighborhoods.

12. Where Will the Business Come From?

McDonald's is projecting a 5.3 percent sales increase. With the fast-food market increasing 4.4 percent and the number of McDonald's outlets projected to increase 3 percent, the goal should be achievable if McDonald's can hold onto the loyalty of its current customer base.

McDonald's two key customers are children, due to their ability to bring the entire family to McDonald's, and adults who eat out without children. The advertising and promotional programs directed toward children this year are similar to past years' programs and should produce similar sales results.

This year McDonald's doesn't have its usual menu changes that have held market share in the adult market; instead, the game promotions, whole wheat buns, and fourth-quarter nostalgia program need to do this. All three programs have indicated they can increase sales 5 to 7 percent during consumer tests. This increase should compensate for the absence of a new menu item.

13. Timetable—1st Quarter

In the timetable below, it is assumed McDonald's will give outlets three-weeks' notice prior to running a program.

Action Item	Key Dates	Quantity	Cost
January:			
Ads for children's programs	All month	250	$15,000,000
Ads for game promotion	All month	400	25,000,000
Implement increased appearances			
of Ronald McDonald	Jan. 15		250,000
Promotional displays	Jan. 2	60,000	1,000,000
New Happy Meal theme	Jan. 25		100,000
Market research contest	Jan. 20		50,000
Promotional prizes	All month	50,000	5,000,000
February:			
Ads for children's programs	All month	250	15,000,000
Ads for game promotion	All month	400	25,000,000
McDonald's high school all-			
star basketball games	Feb. 25	10	1,000,000
New Happy Meal theme	Feb. 25		100,000
Promotional prizes	All month	50,000	5,000,000
March:			
Ads for children's programs	All month	250	15,000,000
Ads for game promotions	All month	400	25,000,000
McDonald's tennis tournament	March 15	1	500,000
Introduce support materials			
to regional co-ops	March 15		1,000,000
New Happy Meal theme	March 25		100,000
Promotional prizes	All month		7,500,000

Although I have omitted it here, in an actual marketing plan, the timetable would continue in a similar manner for the remaining three quarters of the year.

14. Key Risks

For the first time in four years, McDonald's doesn't have a major new product. It's not certain that this plan will have enough impact to overcome this absence.

Burger King and Wendy's have both failed to introduce new products or promotional programs. Both companies are desperate and one or both may introduce a major program that McDonald's has not foreseen.

McDonald's may not be able to find 300 acceptable outlet locations this year, hurting sales both this year and in the future.

1989—POSSIBLE MARKETING PLAN, HITACHI VCRs

1. Objectives

Sales dollars	$221 million
Gross profit dollars	$57 million
Gross margin percent	28%
Net profit dollars	$6 million
Dollar market share	6.3%

2. Sales History

	1986	1987	1988	1989	1990
Total dollar market size	$3,200	$3,500	$3,360	$3,500	$3,600
Hitachi dollar sales	205	224	201	221	234
Hitachi market share	.4%	.4%	.0%	.3%	.5%

All figures are wholesale dollars, in millions.

3. Market Share Trends*

	1986	1987	1988	1989	1990
RCA	12.0%	12.1%	12.0%	12.0%	12.1%
Sony	11.4	11.6	11.7	11.7	11.7
Panasonic	10.7	10.8	10.9	10.8	10.8
Sharp	9.8	9.7	9.8	9.4	9.4
Sanyo	7.0	7.1	6.7	6.6	6.6

*As noted before, these numbers are not accurate, but representative.

3. Market Share Trends (*continued*)

	1986	1987	1988	1989	1990
Fisher	6.8%	6.8%	6.4%	6.3%	6.4%
Magnavox	6.8	6.7	6.4	6.3	6.3
Hitachi	6.4	6.4	6.0	6.3	6.5
Zenith	6.0	5.8	5.5	5.8	5.8

4. Commentary

The VCR market has stopped growing, and most of the companies in the market are struggling to stay profitable. Like other Japanese companies, Hitachi would like to raise prices because of the strong yen, but can't due to the competitive market and the market entry of low-priced Korean VCRs from Samsung and Goldstar.

While Samsung and Goldstar have yet to capture significant market share, they would quickly penetrate the market if Japanese companies were to increase prices. Hitachi is especially vulnerable to the Korean imports because its success in the past has been due to its strategy of low retail prices and high dealer discounts. Up until the arrival of the Korean imports, Hitachi VCRs often had the lowest prices in a store.

The various brands of VCRs are not perceived to be well-differentiated by consumers. This has given an edge to competitors with high name recognition, such as RCA, Panasonic, and Sony. The lack of product differentiation has forced lesser-known companies such as Hitachi to place marketing emphasis at the point of purchase—retail stores. Because retail stores don't want to carry more than five to eight brands, lesser-known manufacturers constantly fight each other to keep a presence in retail outlets.

While Hitachi's sales have continued to do well, its long-term profitability is questionable. It can't raise prices due to Korean competitors, and at the same time, retailers are demanding bigger discounts. Hitachi needs to establish a defensible position in the market, or it may need to discontinue its VCR product line.

5. Competition

Because VCR products are not differentiated, competitors with similar traits have been grouped together.

Sony/Panasonic. Both Sony and Panasonic have established a superior quality image. They sell in prestigious locations, charge premium prices, and rarely discount their product.

RCA/Magnavox. These two firms have been in the consumer electronics market for a long time. They have used their leverage from other electronics products to penetrate a large number of retail outlets. They have a lower price than Sony and Panasonic and offer their outlets co-op advertising programs.

Fisher/Sharp/Sanyo. These firms are the second tier of consumer electronics companies. They don't have the quality reputation of Sony or Panasonic, nor do they have the distribution clout of RCA or Magnavox. Their products are priced below the first two groups of companies, and they offer substantial discounts to their outlets.

Goldstar/Samsung. These are two Korean companies. To date American consumers are not familiar with their products, and their level of quality is still unknown. The Korean models are priced below all others and represent a real threat to Hitachi.

6. Price Comparison

Prices on comparably equipped, mid-range-priced VCRs:

Sony	$410.00
Panasonic	410.00
RCA	390.00
Magnavox	380.00
Zenith	370.00
Fisher	360.00
Sharp	360.00
Sanyo	355.00
Hitachi	335.00
Goldstar	295.00
Samsung	295.00

The price/value relationship between competitors is difficult to evaluate. All of the VCRs have similar performance features, and price appears to be a function of a company's reputation. Since the products are not differentiated, the consumer may be confused and purchase the brand name he or she prefers.

7. Problems/Opportunities

Problems:

1. Hitachi has poor brand-name recognition with consumers.
2. The Hitachi VCR does not have any distinguishing product features, and Hitachi would have difficulty adding features that couldn't be quickly copied by competitors.
3. Hitachi's number and quality of distributors is lower than most of its competitors.
4. Only 3 percent of Hitachi's distributors consider it an important brand.

Opportunities:

1. None of the second tier of consumer manufacturers has a defensible market position; therefore, Hitachi may be able to replace Sanyo, Fisher, or Sharp in some of their outlets.
2. Customer surveys indicate that most consumers are unhappy with the quality of VCR instruction manuals.
3. Because consumer electronics products retail stores are also facing fierce competition, they would be responsive to any program that would provide an edge against their competitors.

8. Major Thrusts

Hitachi has two issues it needs to address. First, it must establish a defensible market position with both consumers and retail outlets, and second, it must raise prices to restore profit margins.

This year's marketing plan will establish a more defensible position with consumers by meeting their need for greatly improved instructions and with retailers by meeting their need for unique promotional campaigns. Next year Hitachi's market position should improve enough for it to raise prices.

The tactics that will be used to implement these thrusts are:

1. Increase consumers' awareness and support of Hitachi's products by:

   - Introducing easy-to-use operating instructions.
   - Creating in-store displays that highlight the easy-to-use instructions.
   - Producing ad materials for co-op ad programs that focus on Hitachi's easy-to-use instructions.

2. Increase retailers' support for Hitachi's VCRs by:

   - Continuing Hitachi's dealer discount program.
   - Providing in-store displays that help sell Hitachi's VCRs.
   - Developing a dealer introduction program emphasizing the benefits of Hitachi's new instructions.
   - Introducing a co-op advertising program equal to 2 percent of a store's purchases from Hitachi.
   - Running a blitz campaign at stores that sell $50,000 worth of Hitachi VCRs in a year.

9. Minor Thrusts

Hitachi will modify and reprint literature to call attention to the new easy-to-use operating instructions.

10. Positioning Statement

Hitachi is a sophisticated electronics company that will enter electronics-based markets where it can profitably manufacture competitive products.

11. Tactics

Instruction Manual. Outside experts have been hired to work on the instruction manual with the engineering department. Some product modifications are required before the VCR will be easy to use. Those changes are being implemented, and the new model VCR with easy-to-follow instructions will be ready by December 1988. Hitachi will ship the new VCR model for 30 days prior to the new program's introduction, allowing retail stores to clear current-model VCRs from inventory.

Dealer Discounts. Hitachi will run this year's quantity discount program again next year.

Salesforce Training. The salesforce will be trained the week of December 1 to introduce the new program.

24-Hour, Toll-Free 800 Number. Effective February 1, 1989, Hitachi will institute a 24-hour hot line for consumers with VCR problems.

Retail Store Introduction. The retail store introduction program will include the proceeding tactics:

Retailers will be notified December 10, 1988 of the impending VCR model change.

The salesforce will present the new program to each retailer by January 15, 1989.

Retail stores will get a free in-store display on the easy-to-use instructions with the purchase of 10 VCRs.

Retail stores will receive an additional 5 percent promotional discount on all VCRs ordered with a display.

The salesforce will have a videotape for each retailer showing positive customer response to the new VCR and its instructions.

New pocket-size sales brochures will be available for retail salespeople to hand out to their customers.

In-Store Displays. Designed by an ad agency, the displays will be five feet high and have the same message on all four sides. The displays will hold 20 VCRs, use minimum floor space, and attract customer attention.

Blitz Displays. The blitz displays, to be rotated through each blitz store, include videos of people using the Hitachi VCR and their positive response to it, as well as a listing of all the product changes Hitachi made so the VCR would be easy to use.

Co-op Advertising. Retailers will earn 2 percent of their purchases in a co-op advertising fund. The retailer can access his earnings when running an ad program that focuses on Hitachi's new instruction manual. The co-op fund will pay for up to half of the ad's costs.

Public Relations. Press releases introducing the new instructions will be sent to Hitachi VCR retailers' local newspapers. Releases will also be distributed to appropriate magazines.

Retailer Blitz Program. Retailers who commit to purchasing $50,000 worth of Hitachi VCRs are entitled to two one-week blitz periods per year. During the blitz period:

Retailers will earn an additional 5 percent co-op advertising allowance on blitz-period purchases to fund up to 50 percent of blitz-period ads.

Retailers' blitz-period purchases will be discounted an additional 5 percent.

Hitachi sales personnel will work in stores on Saturdays and Sundays with the Hitachi blitz display.

12. Where Will the Business Come From?

Hitachi sales are projected to grow 10 percent in a market that's growing 4 percent. This year's program needs to increase business 6 percent over the market's growth, plus make up for the potentially lost sales to Korean imports.

Hitachi should be able to hit the sales objectives this year because:

Discussions with retailers who were considering dropping Hitachi indicate that this program will cut outlet losses to 2 percent. (Hitachi typically loses 4 to 6 percent of its outlets to competitive brands.)

Preliminary discussions with targeted new outlets indicate that with the new program, Hitachi will increase outlets by 7 percent rather than this year's 5 percent.

A small sample survey found that with the new program, 5 out of 15 current retail customers would make Hitachi one of their five main brands. Currently only 3 percent of retailers include Hitachi in their top five.

13. Timetable

Action Items	Key Dates	Quantity	Cost
December 1988:			
Sales training	Dec. 1		$125,000
Video for retailers	Dec. 1		85,000
New store displays	Dec. 20	10,000	300,000
New operating instructions	Dec. 30	30,000	150,000
Hitachi blitz displays	Dec. 30	100	500,000
New retailer sales collateral	Dec. 30	250,000	125,000
Other promotional literature	Dec. 30	250,000	125,000
1st Quarter 1989:			
Co-op advertising support			
materials	Jan. 15		100,000
Introduce toll-free			
800 number	Jan. 30		15,000
Co-op ad expenses*	Jan. 30		80,000
First blitz campaigns	Feb. 15	50	100,000
Co-op ad expenses	Feb. 28		180,000
Blitz campaign	March 15	50	100,000
Co-op ad expenses	March 30		180,000
2nd Quarter 1989:			
Reprint instruction manuals	April 15	30,000	60,000
Blitz campaign	March 15	50	100,000
Co-op ad expenses	April 30		180,000
Blitz campaign	May 15	50	100,000
Co-op ad expenses	May 30		180,000
Blitz campaign	June 15		100,000
Co-op ad expenses	June 30		180,000
3rd Quarter 1989:			
Reprint instruction manuals	July 15	30,000	60,000
Blitz campaign	July 15	50	100,000
Co-op ad expenses	July 30		180,000
Blitz campaign	Aug. 15	50	100,000
Co-op ad expenses	Aug. 30		180,000
Blitz campaign	Sept. 15	50	100,000
Co-op ad expenses	Sept. 30		180,000
4th Quarter 1989:			
Reprint instruction manual	Oct. 15	30,000	60,000
Reprint sales collateral	Oct. 15	100,000	18,000
Reprint promotional			
literature	Oct. 15	100,000	18,000
Blitz campaign	Oct. 15	50	100,000
Co-op ad expenses	Oct. 30		180,000
Blitz campaign	Nov. 15	50	100,000
Co-op ad expenses	Nov. 30		180,000
Blitz campaign	Dec. 15	50	100,000
Co-op ad expenses	Dec. 30		180,000

*Co-op expenses will run 1 percent of sales instead of 2 percent because some retailers won't run co-op advertising, and others won't use their entire co-op earnings.

14. Key Risks

A competitive manufacturer may introduce a major new feature.

Competitors may quickly copy the easy-to-use instructions; however, this risk is minimal because the easy-to-use instructions also required several product modifications.

Fisher, Sanyo, and Sharp may offer large discounts to their retailers to protect market share. It's unlikely, however, that they will take this action because due to the strong yen, all three would be unprofitable with an additional price discount.

Retailers may not be willing to pay for half the costs of Hitachi-oriented ads; however, retailer surveys have indicated initial retailer support for co-op advertising. If retailers' first programs are unsuccessful, they may withdraw their support.

CHAPTER 12

MARKETING PLANS OF STRUGGLING COMPANIES

The first market plan belongs to Technical Test Products, a small company that doesn't have the financial resources to duplicate the technological advances of its competitors. The plan discusses how Technical Test Products can change its target market and then realign its sales strategy to compensate for customers' perception that the company's products have dated technology.

The second company highlighted here, The Paper Outlet, sells paper goods for parties. It is a small store up against a much larger and better-known competitor, and has been unable to develop a customer base. This plan deals with The Paper Outlet's efforts to restructure its product so it complements rather than competes with its competitor's.

Finally the chapter focuses on the professional practice of Dr. Johnson, a 30-year-old dentist who has purchased a retiring dentist's practice. Dr. Johnson's father, who financed the purchase, is also a dentist and has a practice three miles away. For this reason, Dr. Johnson's father doesn't want him to do any advertising. This plan deals with how a young dentist can use inside-out marketing tactics to build a patient base.

1989 MARKETING PLAN—TECHNICAL TEST PRODUCTS

1. Objectives

Sales dollars	$2.58 million
Gross profit dollars	$1.175 million
Gross margin percent	45.5%

Net profit dollars $22,000
Dollar market share   7.1%

2. Sales History

	1986	1987	1988	1989	1990
Total dollar market size (in 000s)	$33,450	$36,310	$35,250	$36,340	$36,370
Technical Test Products dollar sales (in 000s)	2,695	2,725	2,400	2,580	2,605
Technical Test Products market share	7.6%	7.5%	6.8%	7.1%	7.1%

3. Market Share Trends

	1986	1987	1988	1989	1990
Measuretech	47.3%	48.5%	49.6%	49.5%	49.5%
Stuebins	42.2	42.5	42.2	42.0	42.0
Technical Test Products	7.6	7.5	6.8	7.1	7.1

4. Commentary

While Technical Test Products sells to a wide variety of industries, its strongest market has always been companies that do gold plating. In the past, this has accounted for 85 percent of Technical Test Products' sales.

Technical Test Products' two competitors are Measuretech and Stuebins. Until recently, all three manufacturers needed customers to buy auxiliary equipment, including microscopes, radius measurement systems, and density calibrators in order to have a complete, working system. The auxiliary equipment was available through all three competitors.

In 1987, Measuretech and Stuebins introduced integrated systems that didn't require auxiliary equipment. The integrated systems cost 20 percent less and were easier to use than their earlier systems. The integrated systems also worked better than Technical Test Products' system in gold plating applications. Technical Test Products, however, does not have the financial resources to introduce an integrated product.

Although both competitors made inroads into Technical Test Products' market share position in 1988 and threaten to take away more market share in 1989, Technical Test Products still has two advantages over the competition. First, the new systems don't have the same flexibility as the old nonintegrated system. Technical Test Products' system will work better in some specialized applications. Unfortunately the difficult-to-do applications are spread over a wide variety of industries. Second, Technical Test Products' salesforce has more technical competence and can better handle difficult sales calls than its competitors' salesforces.

5. Competition

Measuretech. Measuretech has been in business for more than 50 years, and over 65 percent of all systems in use are Measuretech's. Measuretech has 18 salespeople across the country and advertises heavily. Its products have a better-quality reputation than Stuebins', and it provides excellent customer service and technical support.

Stuebins. Stuebins has been in business about 10 years. The founder was a former sales manager at Measuretech. Stuebins doesn't advertise as much as Measuretech, and its quality, customer service, and technical support are slightly inferior to Measuretech's. Stuebins' strong points are, first, that it routinely brings customers to San Diego for a two-day factory tour and, second, that it is willing to discount its prices to beat Measuretech in bid situations.

6. Price Comparison

These prices are effective October 1, 1988. Technical Test Products' price is for a complete system, including auxiliary equipment, and reflects the 10 percent cost savings the purchasing department has secured. Measuretech's and Stuebin's prices are for their integrated systems.

Technical Test Products	$28,500
Measuretech	$26,000
Stuebins	$25,750

Customers currently feel that Technical Test Products' price is high compared to its competition because its product is outdated and difficult to use.

7. Problems/Opportunities

Problems:

1. Customers have lost sight of the value of Technical Test Products' system.
2. Technical Test Products is too small to advertise enough to communicate a new positioning statement.
3. Technical Test Products' system is the best available for only a small percentage of customers in a wide variety of markets.
4. The company's salesforce morale is low.

Opportunities:

1. There are some market applications where Technical Test Products' equipment works better than the competition's.
2. Customers know Technical Test Products offers excellent quality and technical backup.

8. Major Thrusts

This year's thrust is to reposition Technical Test Products from a company that specializes in gold platings to a company that can solve difficult problems. The thrust will be executed in five ways:

1. Keep the total system price at a 10 percent premium over Measuretech's and Stuebin's prices, emphasizing that Technical Test Products' system can perform in applications where competitors' systems can't.
2. Change the marketing slogan to "Solving difficult problems."
3. Run an intensive three-month ad campaign, communicating the new slogan to customers.
4. Develop an application insurance plan, guaranteeing that Technical Test Products will solve customers' future application problems.
5. Change the company's sales techniques. Instead of trying to be one of the first companies to call on a customer, Technical Test

Products will call last, and only when the customer feels that Measuretech's and Stuebins' systems are inadequate.

9. Minor Thrusts

1. Change the product catalog from 10 to 75 product configurations to emphasize how Technical Test Products can develop the right system for every application.
2. Modify all product literature, highlighting the company's new theme, "Solving difficult problems."

10. Positioning Statement

Technical Test Products provides a completely customized system for difficult applications in the process control environment.

11. Tactics

Ad Campaign.   A full-page ad will run in each of the test industry's four major journals in March, April, and June promoting Technical Test Products' capability of solving difficult problems.

Promotions.   At the major test products convention in May, Technical Test Products will pass out Sherlock Holmes hats with the slogan "Solving difficult problems." The hats will also be distributed to the salesforce for customers who don't attend the convention.

Price Action.   Technical Test Products will keep its 10 percent premium price for two reasons:

1. A higher price clearly indicates the benefit of Technical Test Products' customized systems.
2. Technical Test Products' salesforce is too small to call on more than 15 percent of the potential prospects. Placing the price 10 percent above competition will help the salesforce screen out customers who feel a Measuretech or Stuebins system will work adequately in their application. Only customers who feel they are not getting adequate results from the competitors' systems will want to investigate a system priced at a 10 percent premium.

Marketing Slogan.   The marketing slogan will be changed on

March 1, 1989 from "Experts in measuring gold platings" to "Solving difficult problems." The new slogan will be included in the ad campaign.

Conventions. Technical Test Products will expand to four booths at the test products convention in May. It will also have a large cocktail party the first night of the convention to help introduce the new marketing thrusts.

Public Relations. Press releases will be sent out April 1, 1989 announcing product-line changes and Technical Test Products' capabilities in custom-designed systems.

Application Insurance. Technical Test Products will offer application insurance for either $1,000 per year or $5,000 for the lifetime of its product, guaranteeing that a Technical Test Products' applications expert will develop procedures for new customer applications.

Salesforce Training. All salespeople will receive training in January. The training will cover the strategy outlined below:

When customers request a demonstration, the salesforce will first ask for a sample.

If the customer's application can be met only by Technical Test Products' system, the salesperson will do the demonstration.

If the salesperson is not sure if Measuretech's or Stuebins' equipment will work, the salesperson will wait until the customer has seen competitive demonstrations. If the customer is not completely satisfied with the competitive systems, a Technical Test Products salesperson will do a sales demonstration.

If a salesperson knows a competitive product will work well, Technical Test Products will not do a demonstration.

Sales Literature. All sales literature will be revamped in January and February, repositioning Technical Test Products as the company that solves difficult testing problems.

12. Where Will the Business Come From?

One million dollars of Technical Test Products' sales comes from customers replacing part of a Technical Test Products' system or customers who are duplicating a system already in place. These sales should continue as customers do not like to have two different systems in use for the same application.

About $500,000 in sales comes from foreign markets where both Measuretech and Stuebins have poor sales representation. Technical Test Products should hold this business.

The remaining $1.1 million in sales will have to come from the new thrust. Over the last three years, the average percentage of prospects with difficult problems has been 10 percent. Technical Test Products expects to be able to sell 30 percent of the difficult applications to obtain 1.1 to 1.2 million in sales. A 30 percent closing rate is in line with Technical Test Products' previous closing rate in the gold plating industry.

13. Timetable

Action Items	Key Dates	Quantity	Cost
Reprint literature	Jan.–Feb.	15,000	$20,000
Salesforce training	Jan.		3,000
Increase product line to			
include 75 options	Feb.		15,000
Ad campaign	March	4	16,000
Ad production	March	1	5,000
Ad campaign	April	4	16,000
Public relations campaign	April		500
Introduce application insurance	April		5,000
Introduction party at the			
test products convention	May	1	10,000
Ad campaign	June	4	16,000

14. Key Risks

The ad campaign may not run long enough to effectively communicate the new thrust to customers. A contingency fund is available, if needed, to run the ad campaign three more months.

Prospects may have too many out-of-the-ordinary applications that the applications department won't know how to do. Research and development has made solutions for these applications its top priority.

Customers may still consider Technical Test Products' system outdated. A new housing for the product will be introduced at the May convention to minimize this risk.

1989 MARKETING PLAN—THE PAPER OUTLET

1. Objectives

Sales dollars	$185,000
Gross profit dollars	$64,750
Gross margin percent	35%
Net profit dollars	$5,000
Market share	33%

2. Sales History

	*1986**	*1987*	*1988*	*1989*	*1990*
The Paper Outlet dollar sales	$35,000	$155,000	$145,000	$185,000	$205,000
The Paper Outlet market share	8.0%	24.3%	20.0%	23.0%	23.0%

*Store opened in October 1986.

3. Market Share Trends

	1986	*1987*	*1988*	*1989*	*1990*
Party Time U.S.A.	92.0%	75.7%	80.0%	77.0%	77.0%
The Paper Outlet	8.0	24.3	20.0	23.0	23.0

The Paper Outlet has only one party goods competitor—Party Time U.S.A. Party Time U.S.A.'s sales are growing at a 20 percent per year rate, according to two former employees. In 1987 Party Time U.S.A.

expanded its store by 50 percent. Its sales are estimated to be about $750,000 per year. Party Time U.S.A.'s target market is about twice as large as The Paper Outlet's, leaving The Paper Outlet's market share at approximately 20 percent. The Paper Outlet's share dropped 4 percent between 1987 and 1988 due to Party Time U.S.A.'s store expansion.

4. Commentary

The Paper Outlet went into business in late 1986, locating in one of the two neighborhoods served by Party Time U.S.A. The Paper Outlet's owners thought they would be successful because the Party Time U.S.A. store was one and a half miles from the neighborhood.

But while The Paper Outlet has continued to struggle, Party Time U.S.A. has been growing. The reasons for The Paper Outlet's slow sales are:

Party Time U.S.A. is in a large warehouse and has a large inventory. The Paper Outlet is in a much smaller building and has 25 percent of the inventory of Party Time U.S.A. Customers don't mind driving the extra distance to buy from Party Time U.S.A.'s larger inventory.

Customers like Party Time U.S.A. and aren't interested in switching to a new store.

Customers aren't sure what kind of a store The Paper Outlet is. Only 20 percent of the people in the neighborhood realize it sells paper goods for parties. Few people remember the ads The Paper Outlet had been running in the local paper.

5. Competition

Party Time U.S.A. Party Time U.S.A. opened in 1982 and was a success from the start. Besides its large inventory, Party Time U.S.A.'s other strong features include: a large, noticeable sign; low prices; a well-designed store layout; and attractive window displays.

Party Time U.S.A. advertised the first two years it was in business, but now spends most of its marketing efforts on improving the store's layout.

Other Competition. Other stores in the area, such as grocery and department stores, also sell party goods. But party goods make up only a small part of their merchandise, and their inventory and prices are inferior to both The Paper Outlet's and Party Time U.S.A.'s.

6. Price Comparison

The Paper Outlet has adjusted its prices from 5 percent below to 10 percent above Party Time U.S.A.'s prices; there has not been a noticeable difference in sales at the various price points. People apparently shop at the store with the largest inventory or the store closest to their home rather than at the store with the lowest prices. Currently The Paper Outlet's prices are 5 percent above Party Time U.S.A.'s prices.

7. Problems/Opportunities

Problems:

1. The Paper Outlet's owners have only $25,000 left to invest in the store. If sales don't increase within 12 months, they will close the store.

Opportunities:

1. The Paper Outlet is in an upper-middle-class neighborhood where residents spend a considerable amount of money on their parties.
2. The Paper Outlet is located in a strip mall that draws customers from a larger market than the immediate neighborhood.
3. The Paper Outlet hasn't established a reputation, so it could change its emphasis without losing market momentum.

8. Major Thrusts

The Paper Outlet will reposition itself this year from a party goods paper store to a store with fantastic party themes. The steps the store will take are:

1. Change the name of the store to Fantastic Parties.
2. Change the store layout from plate and cup groupings to great party themes, such as solve-the-mystery and belly dancing parties.

3. Change the marketing slogan from "Discount paper goods" to "The store for unusual, fun, and exciting parties."
4. Develop a list of clowns, fortune tellers, magicians, belly dancers, and other unusual entertainers as a resource list for party planning. Party themes will be created around these entertainers.
5. Run an extensive public relations campaign in local newspapers.
6. Run ads in local newspapers and on the radio promoting Fantastic Parties' themes. Three billboard ads will also be used.

9. Minor Thrusts

None.

10. Positioning Statement

Fantastic Parties is a store with new and unique party themes. This is a change from last year's positioning statement that The Paper Outlet was the neighborhood's most convenient party goods paper outlet.

11. Tactics

New Sign. The new Fantastic Parties sign is being designed by a graphics artist to be as large as township ordinances allow.

Ad Campaign. Fantastic Parties will buy space on three area billboards. Newspaper and radio ads targeted at 35- to 50-year-old neighborhood residents will also run during March, April, and May.

Store Layout. The store's new layout will reflect party themes.

Resource List. The party-planning resource list will be developed in cooperation with various entertainment agents in the area.

Party Merchandise. One of the store owners has visited several New York party stores and contacted several games manufacturers to find vendors for 25 party themes.

Funding. Fantastic Parties requires $50,000 in funding, $25,000 from the owners and $25,000 from a bank. This funding has already been secured.

   Public Relations Campaign. The owners will arrange to talk with all local newspaper entertainment editors to generate interest in articles about Fantastic Parties. The owners also plan to host a party for the editors when the store layout changes.

12. Where Will the Business Come From?

The strip mall in which Fantastic Parties is located draws customers from an area with 14,000 households. The owners of Fantastic Parties have talked to friends and surveyed 100 area households, and they feel the business will be divided as follows:

   $72,000 from children's parties. Households in the area host about 6,000 children's parties per year. Fantastic Parties' surveys indicate that it will sell a party package with an average price of $80 for 15 percent or 900 of those parties.

   $110,000 from adult parties. Area households host 10,000 adult parties per year. Surveys indicate that 10 percent or 1,000 party hosts will buy an average party package of $110.

   $3,000 in miscellaneous sales. This number is lower than the expected $20,000 because the owners are not certain their children's and adult party numbers are accurate.

13. Timetable

Action Items	Key Dates	Quantity	Cost
Funding secured	Jan. 10		$50,000
New inventory	March 1		$16,300
Store layout complete	March 1		10,000
Introduction of new party concept to local editors	March 1		500
New sign	March 1		3,000
Ad campaign—newspapers and radio	March	25	4,000
Three billboard ads	April 1	3	8,000
Public relations stories released	April 15	4	200
Ad campaign	April	25	4,000
Ad campaign	Sept.	25	4,000

14. Key Risks

The ad campaign won't increase sales enough to pay for higher expenses.

Party Time U.S.A. will duplicate the program. The risk is minimized because Fantastic Parties is targeting parties of less than 30 people while Party Time U.S.A.'s primary focus is larger parties.

Fantastic Parties won't be able to develop enough new party themes. One owner's top priority is to develop 5 to 10 new party themes per year.

1989 MARKETING PLAN—DR. JOHNSON, D.D.S.

1. Objectives

Gross profit dollars	$100,000
Net profit dollars	$40,000
Dollar market share	10%

2. Sales History

	1986	1987	1988*	1989	1990
Dr. Johnson's dollar sales	75,000	65,000	65,000	100,000	100,000

*Dr. Johnson purchased the practice in late 1988.

3. Market Share Trends

Dr. Johnson is not sure of the past market shares of various practices. The market has changed considerably over the last three years with the addition of a dental clinic and the practice of Doctors Mills and Caswell. Dr. Johnson has estimated current market shares to be:

	1988
Doctors Mills and Caswell	24.0%
The Dental Clinic	20.0
Dr. Abrahms	20.0
Dr. Johnson, Sr.	16.0
Dr. August	10.0
Dr. Johnson	10.0

4. Commentary

Dr. Johnson recently purchased, with the help of his father, a retiring dentist's practice. For the last two years, Dr. Johnson had been practicing with his father, but he is still relatively unknown in the neighborhood.

Dr. Johnson's acquired patients are mostly older people. The retiring dentist had not kept up his patient load over the last five years and had not attracted any of the younger residents that had moved into the neighborhood.

The neighborhood around Dr. Johnson's practice is 50 years old and changing rapidly. Young families are replacing older residents as they die or retire. The new practices of The Dental Clinic and Doctors Mills and Caswell both appeal to the young families moving into the neighborhood.

Since Dr. Johnson's father does not want him to advertise, Dr. Johnson must hold on to his older patients and develop a new patient base among the people moving into the area while advertising only in the Yellow Pages.

5. Competition

Doctors Mills and Caswell. The two dentists, in their mid-30s, opened their practice two years ago. They have used the following tactics to achieve success:

They have placed a special emphasis on children by setting up a special children's room and by giving out balloons and small toys.

They have been active in the community, giving speeches at schools, writing columns for the local newspapers, and joining several civic groups.

They are open nontraditional hours, including evenings and Saturdays. The two doctors are able to stay open 65 hours a week by splitting office hours.

The Dental Clinic. The Dental Clinic opened three years ago. At first its strategy was to offer extended hours and lower prices; last year The Dental Clinic raised its prices to the area's average. While at first successful, the clinic has had trouble keeping dentists on staff. The Dental Clinic has been losing patients who prefer to see the same dentist every visit.

Dr. Abrahms. Dr. Abrahms has been in practice 20 years and has one associate, Dr. Sartar. The practice has a loyal patient base, and many of Dr. Abrahms' patients return to him after they leave the neighborhood.

Dr. Johnson, Sr. Dr. Johnson, Sr., has been in practice 30 years, has always lived in the neighborhood, and has a loyal customer base.

Dr. August. Dr. August is 70 years old and thinking of retiring. He has a small, loyal customer base among older patients. This might be the doctor that some of Dr. Johnson's patients prefer to switch to, but at this time, Dr. August is not taking any new patients.

6. Price Comparison

All of the area's dentists have similar prices except Dr. Abrahms and Dr. Johnson, Sr., whose prices are 5 to 10 percent higher than the area's average.

7. Problems/Opportunities

Problems:

1. Most of Dr. Johnson's neighborhood friends are patients of his father.
2. The older patients in Dr. Johnson's practice are apprehensive about being treated by such a young dentist.
3. The equipment in Dr. Johnson's office is old and looks outdated to younger patients.

4. Doctors Mills and Caswell are established as the preferred dentists for people moving into the neighborhood.

Opportunities:

1. Some of Dr. Johnson's patients have relatives moving back into the neighborhood.
2. Some of The Dental Clinic's dissatisfied patients are looking for a new dentist. Dr. Johnson's practice is only one block from The Dental Clinic, and he may be able to pick up some of these patients.

8. Major Thrusts

Dr. Johnson has two thrusts this year: first, to hold his current base of older patients, and second, to attract new, younger patients. He plans on implementing each thrust by using various tactics:

1. Tactics for keeping current patients:

   - For one operatory, buy new dental equipment that is specifically designed for older patients.
   - Issue a newsletter every three months to all older patients on file, explaining Dr. Johnson's changes that make an older patient's dental visit more pleasant.

2. Tactics for attracting new patients:

   - Install a new, easily noticed sign.
   - Redecorate the office so it looks modern.
   - Join several civic groups.
   - Offer free X-ray coupons for relatives and friends of current patients.

9. Minor Thrusts

Dr. Johnson will take several steps to help ensure that patients are treated in a friendly manner.

1. Dr. Johnson and his staff will attend a seminar by the local dental society on how to project a friendly attitude toward patients.
2. Dr. Johnson will order new pamphlets for patient education from the American Dental Association.

3. Dr. Johnson will hire a consultant to set up his staff to quickly handle insurance claims.

10. Positioning Statement

Dr. Johnson's dental practice appeals to all neighborhood residents.

11. Tactics

New Equipment. Dr. Johnson will purchase dental equipment that allows older patients to be treated while sitting at a 45-degree angle rather than lying flat, removing one of the major causes of older patients' discomfort. Dr. Johnson will also instruct patients to alert him any time they feel pain.

Newsletter. Dr. Johnson will send out a newsletter to older patients every three months, explaining how his office reduces patients' fear of dentistry.

New Sign. Currently Dr. Johnson's sign has the retired dentist's name on it and is not noticeable. The new sign will be easily seen by people leaving The Dental Clinic.

Redecorating the Office. Dr. Johnson is closing the office for a week so he and his wife can paint and wallpaper every room. Dr. Johnson has also purchased new waiting room furniture and new staff uniforms.

Civic Groups. Dr. Johnson will join the Rotary Club, the local chapter of the Democratic Party, and the Chamber of Commerce.

Coupon Program. Dr. Johnson will offer coupons for free X-rays to every current patient for use by the patient's relatives or friends. The coupons would be good only on a patient's first visit.

12. Where Will the Business Come From?

Dr. Johnson's projected income will be divided as follows:

$55,000 will come from the retired dentist's regular patient base. These patients visit the dentist once or twice per year and are steady customers. Dr. Johnson expects to lose some of these patients, accounting for the $10,000 drop from the 1988 revenue.

About $15,000 will come from reactivating former patients. The retired dentist had stopped sending out notices to past patients, reminding them that they were due for another appointment. Dr. Johnson's father indicated that Dr. Johnson should be able to generate $15,000 from the old patient base.

Patients who want a change from The Dental Clinic will generate about $15,000. Dr. Johnson has been acquiring one or two new patients a week from The Dental Clinic since he added evening and weekend hours. He expects to add two patients a week from The Dental Clinic with the new sign.

Finally $15,000 will come from the coupon program. Dr. Johnson has asked his current patients if they have friends or relatives who might be interested in a free X-ray coupon. Over 30 percent have answered yes. If 25 percent of his patients pass out one coupon, Dr. Johnson will receive $15,000 in new revenue.

13. Timetable

Action Items	Key dates	Quantity	Cost
Staff will attend seminar on projecting a friendly image.	Jan.	1	$ 775
Order patient education pamphlets	Jan.	3,000	450
Install new sign	Jan.	1	1,500
Redecorate office	Jan. 10		2,500
Hire consultant for insurance procedures	Feb.		700
Initiate coupon program	Feb. 15		500
Install new equipment for older patients	Feb. 28	4	12,000
Send out mailing to past patients	Feb. 28	650	500
Send out first newsletter	March	875	400
Join first civic group	March		
Send out second newsletter	June	875	400
Join second civic group	June		
Send out second mailing to past patients	June	650	200
Join third civic group	Aug.		
Send out third newsletter	Sept.	875	400
Send out fourth newsletter	Dec.	875	400

14. Key Risks

More current patients will leave Dr. Johnson than expected.
The Dental Clinic will initiate an aggressive marketing campaign to regain lost patients.

The coupon program will not produce expected results. The program's effectiveness has not been tested.

CHAPTER 13

MARKETING PLANS OF NEW COMPANIES

Most founders of new businesses have trouble writing their first marketing plan—not only because they may not know how to write the plan, but also because they have trouble harnessing their optimism. Too often new business owners are so enthralled with their product that they mistakenly assume that they will easily get customers.

Customers are hard to find, and once you've found them, you must struggle to get them to buy—especially from a new company. If you are a new company, be sure to start with the conviction that you will need to work very hard to get customers.

This chapter has the first marketing plans of three new companies. The first, Hibbing Therapy, has been founded by two young engineers who have developed a new passive exercise device for rebuilding muscles in broken legs. The engineers developed the product with the help of an orthopedic surgeon, and feel their product is superior to five competitive products already on the market. The engineers, however, are receiving a cool response from both physical therapists and medical distributors. The company's marketing plan discusses how to use a market introduction program to penetrate a distribution network.

The second company—Peterson and Newman, Consultants—has been founded by two entrepreneurs who have purchased and turned around three failing retail stores. Peterson and Newman have decided to become consultants to struggling retail stores. But despite their past successes, the consultants are finding that prospective customers don't trust them. Their marketing plan, therefore, discusses how to develop a program that builds customer trust.

The final plan focuses on Bob's Plumbing Service. After several conflicts with his former employer, Bob quit his job and decided to start his own plumbing service. Bob has a limited $2,000 initial marketing budget. His marketing plan explains how Bob can use a focused canvassing program to generate a customer base.

1989 MARKETING PLAN—HIBBING THERAPY

1. Objectives

Sales dollars	$300,000
Gross profit dollars	$180,000
Gross margin percent	60%
Net profit dollars	0
Dollar market share	4%

2. Rationale for Sales Projections

The five current suppliers of passive leg exercisers, machines that move legs in a motion similar to riding a bicycle to build muscle strength, have sales of $7.5 million per year. Their equipment is limited to treating one leg at a time while Hibbing Therapy's equipment can treat both legs at once. The orthopedic surgeon who originally suggested Hibbing Therapy's product feels that a minimum of 20 percent of hospitals and physical therapists would prefer equipment capable of treating both legs.

The engineers will start marketing their equipment in the northeastern states from Massachusetts to Virginia, an area with one third of the total market. Therefore, Hibbing Therapy should be able to achieve a market share of one third of 20 percent, or 6.6 percent. The engineers projected the market share at 4 percent because it will take them six months to introduce the product into all of the targeted states.

3. Market Share Trends

	1986	1987	1988	1989	1990
R&M Therapeutic Equipment	46.0	43.0	41.0	39.0	34.0
Orthopedic Equipment Corp.	16.0	20.0	23.0	25.0	27.0
Grayson's	20.0	18.0	16.0	14.0	12.0
Butler Medical Products	14.0	13.0	12.0	10.0	9.0
U.S. Hospital Equipment	4.0	6.0	8.0	8.0	10.0
Hibbing Therapy	0	0	0	4.0	8.0

4. Commentary

Two years ago, an orthopedic surgeon needed a passive leg exerciser for an older patient who had broken both legs. He approached two engineers in his neighborhood, who developed an exerciser for the surgeon. When the surgeon and two of his colleagues liked the exerciser and saw a market for it, the engineers started Hibbing Therapy.

The engineers have had several exploratory discussions with medical distributors. Although the distributors had some initial interest in selling the exerciser, that faded when the product received a lukewarm reception from physical therapists.

Physical therapists didn't see a value in the product. They felt two broken legs was a rare occurrence, and when it did happen, the legs could be exercised one at a time.

The medical distributors are already carrying three and sometimes four brands of passive exercise equipment. They do not want to add another brand unless there is a compelling reason.

The orthopedic surgeon who originally suggested the exerciser still feels a two-leg model is essential because a one-leg model is uncomfortable for older patients recovering from broken legs. The surgeon emphasizes that younger people don't generally need passive exercise because, unlike older people's, their leg muscles are still strong enough to walk on after eight weeks of non-use.

5. Competition

R&M Therapeutic Equipment.   R&M has always been the market leader in physical therapy equipment. R&M started losing market share six years ago when four of R&M's top engineers left and started Orthopedic Equipment Corporation.

Orthopedic Equipment Corporation.   Orthopedic Equipment is the technology leader in the passive exercise market, and its market share has grown rapidly as customers have recognized the quality of its products. R&M and Orthopedic Equipment are the two brands that virtually all distributors carry.

Grayson's.   Grayson's is an old, established company selling a broad product line of medical equipment. Its market share has continued to shrink as competitors have focused on specific markets while Grayson's has continued to be a broad-line supplier.

Butler Medical Products.   Butler is another long-time supplier. It did well in the market when there were only three competitors, but has been steadily losing market share to new competitors due to quality problems.

U.S. Hospital Equipment.   U.S. Hospital is the leading supplier of medical equipment. It entered the passive exercise market only four years ago, but it has been able to use its clout with distributors to increase market share.

6. Price Comparison

	Suggested Retail Price
Hibbing Therapy	$8,500
Orthopedic Equipment Corp.	6,300
U.S. Hospital Equipment	6,300
R&M Therapeutic Equipment	6,000
Grayson's	5,800
Butler Medical Products	5,600

Hibbing Therapy's price is $2,200 above its competitors, and medical distributors and physical therapists don't perceive Hibbing's product to be worth the premium. The other competitors in the market have a similar price/value relationship. Orthopedic Equipment's and U.S. Hospital's exercisers are priced a little higher because of their quality reputations. Butler's, Grayson's, and R&M's prices are lower because they either offer outdated technology or poor-quality products.

7. Problems/Opportunities

Problems:

1. Hibbing Therapy has only one product, compared to several for each competitor, to sell through distributors.

2. None of the major distributors has agreed to carry Hibbing Therapy's product line.
3. Hibbing Therapy can't afford an extensive advertising program to convince prospects of the value of a two-leg passive exerciser.

Opportunities:

1. Hibbing Therapy has strong support from three orthopedic surgeons.
2. Hibbing Therapy's prototype product has been successfully used on four patients, and one orthopedic surgeon is convinced that the patients' response was much better with Hibbing Therapy's product than it would have been with a one-leg exerciser.
3. Two patients recovering from broken legs will be ready to start treatment the week of November 1, 1988, at a nearby hospital.

8. Major Thrusts

Hibbing Therapy needs to build market momentum so its product will look like a winner to both distributors and physical therapists. Its thrust is to have major product introduction in Hartford, Connecticut, home of the supportive orthopedic surgeons, to get the product off to a big start. The introduction tactics that Hibbing Therapy plans on using follow:

1. Hibbing Therapy will produce a videotape that includes:

- A new patient using the two-leg exerciser.
- The same patient's discomfort using a one-leg exerciser.
- Brief, positive comments from each of the previous users of the two-leg exerciser.
- Diagrams showing why the two-leg exerciser works better than the one-leg model.
- Statistics showing how often a two-leg exerciser is essential to treatment.
- A patient with one broken leg using the two-leg exerciser.

2. The supportive orthopedic surgeons will give a short presentation on the value of the two-leg exerciser.
3. A tax attorney will give a presentation on how surgeons can benefit from new tax rulings.
4. A top orthopedic surgeon will speak on upcoming changes in orthopedic medicine.

5. A buffet dinner will be offered along with the presentations.
6. All physical therapists and orthopedic surgeons in the area will be invited.
7. Hartford's two major medical distributors will also be invited with the understanding that if the introduction goes well, the distributors will carry Hibbing's product.
8. All patients who have used Hibbing's product will be invited to the introduction.
9. Editors from both local newspapers and medical magazines will receive promotional literature packages along with their invitations.
10. Attendees will be asked to fill out a survey about the new product prior to leaving.

9. Minor Thrusts

Hibbing Therapy will prepare a four-page brochure explaining the benefits of the new two-leg passive exerciser.

10. Positioning Statement

Hibbing Therapy supplies passive exercise equipment for patients who are recovering from broken legs.

11. Tactics

Videotape. The professionally prepared videotape will be used after the introduction to explain to other distributors and end-users the benefits of Hibbing Therapy's new product.

Posters. Posters of pertinent photos and statistics will be created for use both at the introduction and for display at medical distributors.

Promotional Package. The promotional package will be used both for editors and for future distributor introductions.

Market Survey. Data collected from the survey taken at the end of the introduction will be used in the future to show orthopedic surgeons' positive response to the two-leg exerciser. The data will be used for press releases and as a sales tool when Hibbing Therapy expands to new markets.

12. Where Will the Business Come From?

Hibbing Therapy has received a positive response from every one of the 15 orthopedic surgeons to whom it has shown the two-leg exerciser. Those surgeons have convinced Hibbing Therapy that it will get at least a 20 percent market share in any market it can successfully enter.

The three supportive orthopedic surgeons have talked to their colleagues throughout the state and are sure the introduction will be well-attended. The distributors have shown in the past that they will support any product that will sell. The introduction program, though expensive, should generate the type of enthusiasm that will get first local and then other distributors to carry the two-leg exerciser.

13. Timetable

Action Item	Key Dates	Quantity	Costs
Video completed	Jan. 10	1	$15,000
Literature printed	Jan. 10	15,000	10,000
Introduction party	Feb. 1	75	
Invitations			250
Room rental			250
Food/cocktails			2,500
Orthopedic surgeon speaker			1,000
Posters			750
Promotional packages			2,500
Patient honorariums			500
Tax attorney			0
Surveys			200
Door prize			500
Contracts signed with Hartford distributors	March 1		
Contracts signed with three additional distributors	April 1		
Contracts signed with three additional distributors	May 1		
Contracts signed with five additional distributors	June 1		
Contracts signed with 10 additional distributors	July 1		

14. Key Risks

The plan anticipates that distributors will be willing to drop either Grayson's or Butler Products, the two weakest competitors, in order to pick up the Hibbing Therapy line. Distributors might not drop Grayson's or Butler Products if one or the other makes a strong effort to hold its business.

The two-leg exerciser prototype has been tested on only four patients. The product may have unexpected flaws. The engineers cannot afford to be without income during the time required for further field testing.

Orthopedic Equipment engineers observed the two-leg exerciser in use three months ago. Hibbing doesn't have patent protection, and Orthopedic Equipment may be rushing a product to market before Hibbing Therapy can get established.

1989 MARKETING PLAN—PETERSON AND NEWMAN: RETAIL STORE CONSULTANTS

1. Objectives

Sales dollars	$150,000
Net profit dollars	$120,000

2. Rationale for Sales Projections

Peterson and Newman are two entrepreneurs who have made three small, struggling retail stores successful. The entrepreneurs have two contracts, Peterson with a franchiser and Newman with a local, expanding clothing chain. They are starting this business so they can be full-time consultants.

Peterson and Newman's sales projections are based on their desired income for the first year. The sales projections do not include their two current contracts. The consultants feel their market potential is unlimited because of the high number of retail stores that are struggling. Peterson and Newman have given five well-attended speeches in the local area on turning around a retail store. After each speech, two to five retail store owners have asked if Peterson and Newman could help their stores. Peterson and Newman are confident that they will be able to find customers through future speeches.

3. Market Share Trends

There are few retail marketing consultants in Peterson and Newman's area. Some marketing consultants do occasional work for retail stores, and a few retired retail owners offer help on a part-time basis. But for the most part, Peterson and Newman don't have any direct competitors.

4. Commentary

Peterson and Newman's initial consulting efforts have been disasters. Their first two potential clients didn't pursue the consultants after an initial meeting, and two other clients decided not to use Peterson and Newman's suggested strategy.

The consultants have talked to both potential and actual clients to try and understand what they are doing wrong. The points that have come up in these discussions are:

> One client wondered why, since Peterson and Newman were such experts, they didn't open their own retail store.

> Two clients were just holding on, hoping to solve their problems themselves without having to hire Peterson and Newman.

> Both actual clients thought Peterson and Newman didn't give advice that was worth their fees. In both cases, the store owners had previously considered Peterson and Newman's ideas and elected not to implement them.

> One potential client felt Peterson and Newman's business approach was too different than his.

> One client was upset at Peterson and Newman because he felt they were extremely critical of his current efforts.

> One client said he didn't really understand the rationale for Peterson and Newman's action plan and was afraid he would lose control of his business by implementing it.

> Two clients stated they never felt comfortable with Peterson and Newman, though they weren't sure why.

Peterson and Newman realized that all of these comments were indications that they had failed to develop a working relationship with their clients.

Peterson and Newman had initially started their business because they thought struggling retail owners would be happy to take advantage of their advice. But Peterson and Newman now realize that retailers were looking for help, but help from an equal partner, where the retailers' input was just as important as the consultants'.

5. Competition

Marketing Consultants. Some marketing and advertising consultants in the area help retailers create promotions and in-store displays. Their services focus on only that area of the retailers' business, but it is an area where many retailers are not sure what to do.

Retired Retail Store Owners. Their services are usually obtained through a state-run agency. The retired owners generally spend only 10 hours with new store owners, helping them choose a location and showing them how to find the lowest-cost sources of supply. The retired owners work on a volunteer basis and may or may not have experience in the retailers' type of business.

6. Price Comparison

	Range of Typical Fees
Peterson and Newman	$5,000–$15,000
Marketing consultants	$2,000–$ 5,000
Retired retail owners	0

Peterson and Newman were considered overpriced by their two actual clients mainly because the consultants wouldn't accept the retailer's understanding of his problems. Instead the consultants did their own costly analysis, only to come to the same conclusions as the retail owner. This problem should be removed with Peterson and Newman's new strategy of creating a better client/consultant working relationship.

Otherwise Peterson and Newman's premium price is justified as they offer a much wider array of services than the marketing consultants, including personnel, purchasing, inventory, mark-up, and promotional policies. Peterson and Newman's fee is $85 per hour.

7. Problems/Opportunities

Problems:

1. Peterson and Newman haven't yet established the value of their services.
2. Peterson and Newman's $85 per hour fee scares off many potential clients.
3. Peterson and Newman have yet to prove that they can gain the trust of potential clients.

Opportunities:

1. Peterson and Newman receive speaking invitations every six to eight weeks.
2. Peterson and Newman's two current customers have both written testimonial letters.

8. Major Thrusts

Peterson and Newman's thrust this year is to develop close client/consultant working relationships. The planned action steps are:

1. Develop a comprehensive sales presentation that includes:

   • Why Peterson and Newman decided to be consultants.
   • How Peterson and Newman have turned around other retail businesses.
   • An explanation of the value of Peterson and Newman's unique services.

2. Offer an initial consulting session for $200.
3. Emphasize at the start and finish of every client contact that Peterson and Newman's job is to help the client meet his or her objectives, and not to tell the client what to do.
4. Schedule periodic progress meetings to explain to the client what they've been doing and why.
5. Offer two or three options for the client to choose from in all client consultations.

9. Minor Thrusts

Peterson and Newman's minor thrust will be to place its name in front of potential customers in the following ways:

1. Give a minimum of eight speeches throughout the year.
2. Develop and promote a one-day seminar on how to turn around a retail business.
3. Write a monthly column in the local business magazine.

10. Positioning Statement

Peterson and Newman, Consultants provides complete consulting services for retail stores.

11. Tactics

Sales Presentation. The sales presentation is designed to set the stage for a cooperative client/consultant relationship. The presentation has two focuses: first, Peterson and Newman's extensive retailing experience, and second, how the consultants work together with the client to find the best solution.

Initial Consulting Session. This session has three purposes:

1. $200 is a reasonable price for an initial three- to four-hour session, overcoming the client's apprehension about the $85 per hour fee.
2. It allows both the client and consultant to agree on what needs to be done.
3. It allows the client a relatively risk-free method of learning what Peterson and Newman, Consultants has to offer.

Periodic Progress Meetings. Again, these meetings will be designed primarily to keep clients informed so that they feel in control of the consulting process.

One-Day Seminar. Both consultants have enough material from past speeches to offer a one-day seminar. The seminar's promotion should enhance the consultants' image as well as generate sales leads.

Monthly Column. The local business magazine is trying to increase its readership among retail store owners. It has already approached the consultants about writing a monthly column, offering tips to retail store owners.

12. Where Will the Business Come From?

Peterson and Newman need 20 to 30 clients per year to hit their sales target of $150,000. The consultants expect to find the 70 to 85 strong prospects needed to obtain 20 to 30 clients from:

17 interested prospects currently on file from past speeches. Peterson and Newman delayed any prospect follow-up until they developed a new consulting strategy.

20 potential prospects from future speeches.

25 prospects from seminars. This is consistent with the consultants' previous seminar experiences.

20 prospects from their newspaper column. This is consistent with the number of leads the accountant and marketing columnists receive.

Peterson and Newman also think their new consulting strategy will work. The consultants researched the new strategy both by reading four books and by talking with noncompeting consultants in their town. The consultants are fairly confident the new strategy will effectively close 33 percent of their strong prospects.

13. Timetable

Action Item	Key Dates	Quantity	Cost
Sales presentation ready	Jan. 1		
Sales tools	Jan. 1	15	$ 300
Start new consulting strategy	Jan. 1		
Give a speech to a business organization	Feb.		
Give first one-day seminar	April		
Seminar materials	April 1		500
Promotion and advertising	April 1		1,000
Start magazine column	April 20		
Give second speech	May		
Give third speech	June		
Give fourth speech	Aug.		
Give fifth speech	Sept.		
Give second one-day seminar	Oct.		1,000
Give sixth speech	Oct.		
Give seventh speech	Nov.		
Give eighth speech	Dec.		

14. Key Risks

The new strategy may not raise the closing rate to 33 percent. Both consultants are planning on drawing only half a salary the first year in case sales don't hit projected levels.

The number of prospects generated may be lower than expected. Peterson and Newman are prepared to run a direct mail campaign in May if the number of prospects is too low.

1989 MARKETING PLAN—BOB'S PLUMBING SERVICE

1. Objectives

Sales dollars	$35,000
New profit dollars	$28,000
Dollar market share	25%

2. Rationale for Sales Projections

Bob has worked for two of the three plumbers who serve his suburban township and is now starting his own business. Bob has decided to focus his marketing efforts on the 30-year-old development he lives in, where almost every house has the same two or three plumbing problems. Bob knows from past work experience that this development generates about $140,000 in plumbing business each year. By concentrating exclusively on this development, Bob feels that he will be able to obtain 25 percent of the development's plumbing business.

3. Market Share Trends

	1986	1987	1988	1989	1990
Ace Plumbing	45.0%	55.0%	58.0%	50.0%	46.0%
Jack's Plumbing Service	45.0	35.0	33.0	20.0	16.0
Audubon Plumbing	10.0	10.0	10.0	5.0	3.0
Bob's Plumbing Service	0	0	0	25.0	33.0

4. Commentary

Bob had a disagreement with his former boss and decided to start his own plumbing service. Bob knows that most people choose a plumber either from past experience or through the Yellow Pages. Since he won't be able to get business from either of those sources, Bob needs to create an alternate plan to generate sales.

Bob's friend started a closet remodeling business two years ago, successfully capitalizing on the fact that most of the homes in the township were built from one of five floorplans. The friend developed and priced closet packages for each of the five different floorplans. Then he canvassed the township, introduced himself to residents, and handed each resident the appropriate closet remodeling brochure.

Bob planned on duplicating his friend's strategy. He felt he could make it work for two reasons. First, he was fairly well known in the development from coaching his son's baseball teams, and second, the homes' similar plumbing problems made a package strategy appropriate.

5. Competition

Ace Plumbing. Ace is the largest plumbing service in the area, employing four plumbers. Ace has been in the area the longest and provides prompt, competent service. Its one disadvantage is that customers get a different plumber every visit.

Jack's Plumbing Service. Jack's is on the other side of the township. All Jack's plumbers are relatives of the owner. Jack's is losing market share in the development because one of its plumbers retired, and Jack's has been too busy to provide prompt service.

Audubon Plumbing. Audubon is 10 miles away and typically only gets business when Ace and Jack's are busy. Audubon Plumbing has been in business three years and no longer needs the business in Bob's target development.

6. Price Comparison

All the plumbers in the area charge similar prices. The only exception is Bob, who offers a 10 percent discount on his plumbing packages due to his material cost savings.

7. Problems/Opportunities

Problems:

1. Bob has only $2,000 to promote his business.
2. Residents in the development are not aware that Bob started his own business.
3. Bob won't be able to place an ad in the Yellow Pages for 12 months.
4. Most residents have lived in their homes at least two or three years and already have a plumber.

Opportunities:

1. Jack's Plumbing Service and Audubon Plumbing are both scaling back their service to Bob's target development.
2. The similarity in plumbing problems makes a brochure with predetermined packages of plumbing services appropriate.
3. Bob is fairly well known in the development.
4. Bob is personable and creates a favorable impression in face-to-face sales contacts.

8. Major Thrusts

Bob has two main thrusts: to develop a list of five or six plumbing jobs that would be of interest to the development's residents, and to initiate a canvassing campaign where he will try to meet and leave a brochure with all of the development's 1,400 homeowners.

9. Minor Thrusts

Bob will put his business card on every appropriate bulletin board in the township; he will also advertise, under Services, in the classified section of the local newspaper. Bob will also have a sign with his phone number painted on the side of his van.

10. Positioning Statement

Bob's Plumbing Service specializes in the plumbing needs of the Cannon Run residential development in Swedestown, Pennsylvania.

11. Tactics

Plumbing Packages. Bob will offer the following plumbing packages:

Add a shower in the first-floor powder room.

Install shut-off valves in the second-floor bathroom, in the first-floor powder room, and under the kitchen sink.

Install a laundry tub in the basement laundry room.

Replace the often-leaking drain pipe from the second-floor bathtub.

Install a second outdoor faucet in the back left or right corner of the house.

Replace the water heater with a larger, more efficient unit.

Brochure. Bob will have a two-page, two-color, sales brochure listing the plumbing packages as well as a little information about Bob. The brochure will include a picture of Bob's home's remodeled first-floor powder room.

Canvassing Campaign. Bob plans to stop at each home in the development, introduce himself, and hand out a brochure. Bob plans on canvassing both during the days and in the early evening. If he fails to find anyone home after three visits, Bob will just leave his sales brochure.

12. Where Will the Business Come From?

Bob feels his business will come from four sources:

15 percent from Bob's neighbors and friends of neighbors.

35 percent from people who aren't able to get prompt service from Jack's or Audubon Plumbing. According to a small survey Bob took in the neighborhood, 10 percent of the residents have had trouble getting a plumber to come to their homes. Bob feels that after his canvassing campaign, he will get 40 percent of this business. Ace Plumbing will get the rest.

20 percent from residents that have moved into the development within the last three years and have yet to need a plumber. Bob's survey found that about 15 percent of the residents had purchased their homes within the last three years.

30 percent from residents that want one of Bob's plumbing packages. Bob noticed that surveyed residents were especially interested in converting the first-floor powder room to a second full bath and in adding a basement laundry tub.

13. Timetable

Action Item	Key Dates	Quantity	Cost
Have signs painted on van	Jan.	2	$ 600
Print business cards and invoices	Jan.	2,000	50
Print brochures	Jan.	5,000	1,200
Add a business phone at his home	Jan.		50
Classified ads	Jan.–March	24	100
Classified ads	Apr.–June	24	100
Classified ads	July–Sept.	24	100
Classified ads	Oct.–Dec.	24	100

14. Key Risks

Jack's Plumbing may add a nonfamily plumber to improve its service level; however, this is unlikely since Jack's last two nonfamily plumbers were fired within a week.

Residents may be reluctant to use the services of a new plumber. Bob feels this risk is minimal because his brochure emphasizes his six years of plumbing experience.

Residents won't be willing to undertake the major projects listed in Bob's plumbing packages. This risk is low because many of the residents, with low mortgages obtained 10 to 15 years ago, are now able to take out home equity loans to upgrade their homes.

PART 3 SUMMARY

You should now be ready to go back to Chapter 10 and write your own marketing plan. As you follow the format, remember that it is not meant to be restrictive; you should modify it to better fit your business if necessary. Just be sure your modified version meets the objectives of the original format:

Clearly indicate that the plan is focusing on one or more key marketing elements.

Show that the marketing plan is consistent in its focus on the identified key marketing elements.

Demonstrate that the marketing plan is powerful enough to meet sales and profit objectives.

Contain a timetable for you or someone else to follow throughout the year.

Provide top management or outside investors a quick understanding of what your marketing program will be and why it will work.

INDEX